Praise for *Advancing Immigrant Rights in Houston*

"Houston's experience serves as a roadmap for other new immigrant gateway cities across the United States that are grappling with rapid demographic change and are nested within conflicting and complex national, state, and local political dynamics. In *Advancing Immigrant Rights in Houston*, de Graauw and Gleeson, two highly respected experts in the field, paint a nuanced picture of the 'strange bedfellow' coalitions that achieved hard-won immigrant rights in Houston. They offer lessons that reverberate beyond the nation's fourth largest city."
—MONICA VARSANYI, CUNY, and editor of *Taking Local Control: Immigration Policy Activism in U.S. Cities and States*

"Immigration may be a national issue, but immigrant incorporation is profoundly local. Past studies have often sought to plumb lessons from traditional gateways even as migration flows have reshaped cities and suburbs across the nation. de Graauw and Gleeson flip this script with a painstakingly researched, wonderfully nuanced, and deeply rooted study that starts but does not stay in Houston. Highlighting the complex politics and the unusual alliances needed to make progress on immigrant rights in one of the nation's most politically challenging and demographically diverse metro areas, they offer a guide for what immigrant advocates and allies will encounter and must overcome in the rest of America."
—MANUEL PASTOR, Distinguished Professor of Sociology and American Studies and Ethnicity at the University of Southern California, and coauthor of *Equity, Growth, and Community: What the Nation Can Learn from America's Metro Areas*

Advancing Immigrant Rights in Houston

In the series *Political Lessons from American Cities*,
edited by Richardson Dilworth

ALSO IN THIS SERIES:

Paul G. Lewis and Nicholas J. Marantz, *Regional Governance and the Politics of Housing in the San Francisco Bay Area*
Richardson Dilworth, *Reforming Philadelphia, 1682–2022*
Ann O'M. Bowman, *Reinventing the Austin City Council*

ELS DE GRAAUW AND
SHANNON GLEESON

Advancing Immigrant Rights in Houston

TEMPLE UNIVERSITY PRESS
Philadelphia • *Rome* • *Tokyo*

TEMPLE UNIVERSITY PRESS
Philadelphia, Pennsylvania 19122
tupress.temple.edu

Copyright © 2024 by Temple University—Of The Commonwealth System of Higher Education
All rights reserved
Published 2024

Library of Congress Cataloging-in-Publication Data

Names: De Graauw, Els, author. | Gleeson, Shannon, 1980– author.
Title: Advancing immigrant rights in Houston / Els de Graauw and Shannon Gleeson.
Other titles: Political lessons from American cities.
Description: Philadelphia : Temple University Press, 2024. | Series: Political lessons from American cities | Includes bibliographical references and index. | Summary: "Shows that the advancement of immigrant rights in Houston has necessitated a diverse, and at times unusual, set of governmental and non-governmental actors to collaborate and negotiate difficult compromises"— Provided by publisher.
Identifiers: LCCN 2024006733 (print) | LCCN 2024006734 (ebook) | ISBN 9781439924396 (cloth) | ISBN 9781439924402 (paperback) | ISBN 9781439924419 (pdf)
Subjects: LCSH: Emigration and immigration—Texas—Houston—History—21st century. | Immigrants—Civil rights—Texas—Houston. | Houston (Tex.)—Emigration and immigration—Government policy. | United States—Emigration and immigration—Government policy.
Classification: LCC JV7100.H68 D4 2024 (print) | LCC JV7100.H68 (ebook) | DDC 325.764—dc23/eng/20240408
LC record available at https://lccn.loc.gov/2024006733
LC ebook record available at https://lccn.loc.gov/2024006734

♾ The paper used in this publication meets the requirements of the American National Standard for Information Sciences—Permanence of Paper for Printed Library Materials, ANSI Z39.48-1992

Printed in the United States of America

9 8 7 6 5 4 3 2 1

Contents

	Acknowledgments	vii
	Introduction: Houston and the Local Turn in Immigration	1
1.	Houston's Challenging Context for Advancing Immigrant Rights	7
2.	Between Sanctuary and Enforcement: The Politics of Immigrant Rights in Houston	33
3.	Cautious Optimism: The Future of Immigrant Rights in Houston	64
	Conclusion: Houston's Lessons for Studying Immigrant Rights in Other Cities	80
	Notes	87
	References	91
	Index	109

Acknowledgments

This monograph is the result of two decades of research in Houston through many stages of our academic careers. Over the years, generous support has been provided by Baruch College–CUNY, Cornell University, the National Science Foundation (grants SES-1354115, SES-1445436, and SES-0703399), the Netherlands Institute for Advanced Study, the Professional Staff Congress of CUNY (awards TRADB-42-725, TRADB-45-473, TRADB-48-432, and TRADA-51-606), the University of California at Berkeley, and the University of California at Santa Cruz.

Many research assistants at Baruch College, the CUNY Graduate Center, and Cornell University have contributed to literature reviews and interview data analysis, including Hannah Cho, Adriana Cruz, Yoselinda Mendoza, Jenny Munoz, Amy Saz, and Siqi Tu. We thank Mike Boruta for the cartography, Linda Hallinger for index preparation, and Matt Seidel for expert manuscript editing. We also thank Anat Ronen for allowing us to use her mural art at Blackshear Elementary School in Houston to grace the cover of this book. Finally, we appreciate the feedback and guidance we received from two anonymous reviewers, as well as from Richardson Dilworth and Aaron Javsicas. Finally, we thank all the interview respondents who have participated in this research over the years.

Earlier analyses of our research in Houston have been published in the journals *Critical Sociology* (2021), *Journal of Ethnic and Migration Studies* (2020 and 2023), *Law & Policy* (2023), *Social Problems* (2022), and *Urban Ge-*

ography (2021). Book chapters from these data can also be found in the edited volumes *No One Size Fits All: Worker Organization, Policy, and Movement for a New Economic Age* (LERA Research Volume Series, 2018) and *The City Is the Factory: Social Movements in the Age of Neoliberal Urbanism* (Cornell University Press, 2017).

Advancing Immigrant Rights in Houston

Introduction

*Houston and the Local Turn
in Immigration*

To understand immigration politics in Houston, several of our local contacts said that we needed to meet with Stan Marek. One of the first times we talked to him was in 2009, when one of us drove to a restaurant near Houston's upscale Galleria mall to meet him. Marek arrived in his SUV, dressed in a collared shirt, jeans, and cowboy boots. Marek is not a lawyer, activist, or even politician. Rather, he is one of Houston's most prominent businesspeople and a descendant of Czech immigrants. While driving to a Catholic Charities facility, one of the foci of his community engagement when he is not busy running one of the largest construction companies in Houston, he explained what motivated his work on immigration issues: his Catholic faith and good business sense. While doing research on immigrant rights in Houston over a 15-year span, we met with Marek several times, learning about his advocacy for "sensible" national immigration reform and state and local immigrant rights measures that also promote fair business practices. A lifelong Republican who has the ear of Democratic politicians, receives the ire of right-wing conservatives, and occasionally collaborates with immigrant rights advocates, Marek embodies all that is complicated and perplexing about advancing immigrant rights in Houston.

Houston—the largest city in Texas and the fourth largest in the nation with about 2.3 million residents—is one of the most diverse cities in the United States and has long been a prime destination for international migrants. Mexicans are the city's largest immigrant group, yet Houston is also among the top five destinations for migrants and refugees from several other countries in Latin America, Asia, and, more recently, Africa. Contemporary immigrants and refugees enter a city that is already multiethnic: non-Hispanic White people and African Americans each make up just under a quarter of the city's population and Latinos (some of whom identify as Tejano) nearly half. While international migration is making Houston's population ever more diverse, demography is not destiny. In fact, Houston offers a challenging context for advancing immigrant rights: the city is politically mixed, organizationally underserved, and situated in a notably anti-immigrant state. This leads us to ask: *How have immigrant rights been advanced in this private sector-oriented global city, which is set within a relatively conservative political environment?* This book argues that a diverse, and at times unusual, set of governmental and nongovernmental actors collaborating and negotiating difficult compromises has made possible several advances in immigrant rights in Houston.

This book recounts the contemporary politics of immigrant rights in Houston and, more broadly, the increasing importance of local contexts of reception for enacting and implementing immigration policies in the United States (Filomeno 2017). The prolonged stalemate over comprehensive federal immigration reform has led U.S. cities to create policies responding to their growing immigrant constituencies (Varsanyi 2010). Between 1990 and 2020, the foreign-born population across the United States more than doubled from 19.8 million (8 percent of the population) to 44.9 million (14 percent). While immigrants continue to settle in large and relatively immigrant-friendly gateway cities such as New York City, Chicago, and San Francisco, they are now also making their homes in newer destinations—both central cities and suburbs—with more recent immigration histories, including in southern cities like Atlanta and Washington, DC (Mollenkopf and Pastor 2016; Singer, Hardwick, and Brettell 2008). The increase and significant geographic dispersion of immigrants in recent decades has sparked research that typologizes different city responses to immigration issues, often along a policy continuum from pro- to anti-immigrant (e.g., Pham and Van 2014).

Scholars have also long examined what drives local immigration policymaking, including the importance of local demographic, political, and civic factors. We know that certain local contexts make city officials more open to enacting and implementing pro-immigrant policies—for instance, large immigrant populations (e.g., Huang and Liu 2018; Walker and Leitner 2011), sufficient government resources (e.g., de Graauw 2016), progressive political cultures (e.g., Hopkins 2010; Ramakrishnan and Wong 2010), favorable institutional arrangements (e.g., de Wilde and Nicholls 2021), and active and well-resourced community organizations (e.g., de Graauw and Vermeulen 2016; Steil and Vasi 2014). Other research has demonstrated how state and federal governments can influence local responses to immigrant needs and interests, especially given cities' subordinate position within the hierarchical U.S. federalist system of government (e.g., Provine et al. 2016; Wells 2004). While U.S. cities have notable power and control over land use, policing, education, and housing, their immigrant rights policies cannot contravene state policies or those of the federal government, which has exclusive power over immigration and citizenship issues (Rodríguez 2017).

Urban scholars have studied immigration politics in many different U.S. cities and suburbs, but Houston has received surprisingly little attention. Houston has experienced mass migration since World War II, and today, 29 percent of its population is foreign born. In large part because of sustained economic and refugee migration from Latin America and Asia, Houston's population is currently the most evenly split among the four major ethnoracial groups—non-Hispanic Whites (24 percent), Blacks (23 percent), Latinos (45 percent), and Asians (7 percent)—of any major U.S. city (ACS 2023a). Despite this diversity, Houston remains highly segregated and politically divided. Moreover, longtime observers of the city's population trends describe Houston as a "prophetic city" that portends the nation's demographic future, serving as a bellwether for how other urban centers will respond to immigration-generated diversity (Klineberg 2020a).

Compared to traditional immigrant destinations that tend to be reliably Democratic bastions, Houston's political context is "purple," with the balance of power swaying between Democrats and Republicans. Indeed, local politics in Houston are not easily categorized as either pro- or anti-immigrant. Houston has had Democratic mayors since 1982, though both Republicans and Democrats have been elected to its city council. Most city officials today hold relatively pro-immigrant views, but they have been much more muted in their immigrant advocacy than their colleagues in more progressive gateway cities like New York City and San Francisco. While the Houston police chief has refused to permit officers to apprehend and detain undocumented immigrants simply because of their unauthorized status, other city officials have repeatedly refused to label Houston as a "sanctuary city." Houston, furthermore, has been inconsistent in supporting immigrant services, and leaders who take pride in the city's small-government and business-friendly identity have avoided large public outlays that would draw constituent criticism. In recent history, for example, city officials created and subsequently defunded three centers serving immigrant day laborers (Gleeson 2012). Finally, Houston does have an office dedicated to immigrant and refugee affairs, the Office of New Americans and Immigrant Communities. However, this office—whose name and identity have shifted over the years—has been politically contentious since its 2001 creation and has only two staff members to address the varied needs and interests of the city's 662,000 foreign born (ACS 2023a; de Graauw 2018).

The city of Houston, which is almost entirely located in the now reliably Democratic jurisdiction of Harris County (Ura 2016), is ringed by staunchly conservative suburban and rural counties, where politicians generally favor immigration enforcement over immigrant rights. Republican officials rule the Texas state legislature by a wide margin, adding another layer of conservatism to the region's political landscape. Republican governor Greg Abbott, the state's top executive who is focused on cracking down on undocumented immigration, mobilized the National Guard and has installed deadly buoy barriers in the Rio Grande to block the flow of immigrants into the state. He also joined Florida in sending busloads of migrants out of state to Democratic-run cities elsewhere.

Yet Texas is also a place of contradictions. Despite its staunchly anti-immigrant history, it was also the first to enact—under Republican governor Rick Perry—a state Dream Act in 2001, allowing in-state tuition and state financial aid at public universities and community colleges for eligible undocumented students. Today, this policy faces ongoing attacks from Republican lawmakers (Olivas 2020). Fueled by a hardening political landscape, anti-immigrant policies have become more common in Texas in recent years. In 2014 and 2018, state officials led multistate lawsuits against President Obama's 2012 Deferred Action for Childhood Arrivals (DACA) program, which has offered temporary deportation relief to over 835,000 undocumented youth (DHS 2023b), with the second-largest group of DACA-eligible youth residing in Texas. In 2017, Texas state officials also enacted SB4, a law that resembles Arizona's controversial 2010 "show me your papers" legislation (SB1070) and effectively bans sanctuary cities in the state. In 2020, on the heels of a series of Trump-era federal refugee bans, Governor Abbott vetoed the resettlement of any refugees in Texas. In all, immigrant rights advocates in Houston confront a challenging multilevel political context.

Not only are Houston's politics more conservative compared with other large immigrant gateway cities, but the city's civic infrastructure is also sparser and less developed. Compared with New York City, Chicago, and San Francisco, Houston has relatively fewer nonprofit organizations that can mediate the challenges and opportunities of immigration-driven diversity (de Graauw, Gleeson, and Bada 2020). Instead, business leaders and their organizations are important agenda setters, sources of political clout, and funders that can either move local immigration policies forward or thwart them. For example, the Greater Houston Partnership—the local chamber of commerce—is a powerful actor in Houston politics, as are individual business leaders like Stan Marek. Their interests, however, are unabashedly market based and often clash with the agendas of immigrant rights organizations. This tension has challenged city leaders who want to address the needs of their newest residents while also maintaining a business-friendly environment. And while labor unions have been powerful and vocal allies in the fight to advance immigrant rights in other big cities, Houston-area unions wield little political and policy influence in this "right to work" state (de Graauw and Gleeson 2021a). Overall, the wide dispersion of civic power and the absence of a dominant, powerful local advocacy organization (such as the New York Immigration Coalition or the Coalition for Humane Immigrant Rights of Los Angeles) make Houston a useful case for understanding the full scope of local responses to growing immigrant populations.

This book tells the story of how Houston—a rapidly diversifying, politically mixed, and organizationally underserved city—has advanced immigrant rights in recent years. Rather than follow in the footsteps of more established immigrant gateway cities, Houston has developed a strategy customized to its circumstances: one where a diverse, and at times unusual, set of governmental and nongovernmental actors has had to collaborate and negotiate difficult compromises to realize immigrant rights advances. Our conclusions are based on 196 interviews conducted since 2005 with local government officials, immigrant rights advocates, labor movement staff, faith leaders, philanthropic funders, and business owners (e.g., de Graauw and Gleeson 2021a, 2021b; Gleeson 2012). While centered on Houston, this book illuminates the ways local and multilevel contexts shape how immigrant rights policies and practices are conceived and implemented, and to what end. Indeed, Houston highlights how immigrant rights can be advanced in a place resistant to change yet facing a demographic reality that demands it.

Chapter 1 lays out Houston as a useful case for understanding immigration politics. It discusses the recent history of migration to Houston and how immigrants have contributed to the city's economic development and demographic evolution. Through a multilevel lens, we consider the city's government structure and the mixed political context in which immigrant rights debates take place in the region. Finally, this chapter assesses the city's civic infrastructure, underscoring the relative paucity of nongovernmental actors and institutions focused on advancing immigrant rights. We discuss immigrant-led organizations, faith-based institutions, philanthropic funders, labor unions, and business organizations. Via comparisons to other big U.S. cities, this chapter underscores the unique context that makes realizing immigrant rights in Houston so challenging.

Chapter 2 illustrates how those governmental and nongovernmental immigrant rights advocates have collaborated—sometimes in confrontational ways—as they navigate Houston's challenging demographic, political, and civic landscape. Four cases are discussed: (1) the 2001 creation of a city immigrant affairs office and the precarious efforts to institutionalize this office in ensuing years; (2) how the Houston Police Department and the Harris County Sheriff's Office have navigated calls to support federal immigration enforcement efforts; (3) local public-private partnerships that help Houston's immigrants access federal immigration benefits such as U.S. citizenship and the 2012 DACA program; and (4) the collaborations among labor, immigrant rights, faith, and business leaders—strange bedfellows at best—that culminated in a successful 2013 campaign to combat wage theft.

Chapter 3 reflects on how recent changes in federal and state leadership will continue to shape discussions in Houston around immigration policy. This chapter speculates about the future of immigrant rights in Houston as the city becomes majority Hispanic and as the second generation increasingly enters civic and political life. We also consider the implications of the Democratic Party slowly gaining ground in local elections, as well as the maturation and expansion of Houston's organizational infrastructure for immigrant rights.

Finally, the conclusion offers a road map for studying other U.S. cities and suburbs responding to their growing immigrant populations.

1

Houston's Challenging Context for Advancing Immigrant Rights

Roughly one-third (29 percent) of Houston's 2.3 million residents are foreign born, and two-thirds (67 percent) of them are noncitizens (ACS 2023a). Immigrant-origin diversity in Houston is indicative of where many other parts of the country are projected to head in coming decades: a majority-minority city where no one ethnoracial group dominates. While national immigration policies have focused on border enforcement and restricting rights, Houston's demographic reality has necessitated local policies that instead address immigrant integration, as many new immigrants struggle with low incomes, little formal education, limited proficiency in English, and lack of legal status (Capps, Fix, and Nwosu 2015; Klineberg 2020a).

Despite being a major immigrant gateway, Houston is not a haven for progressive city politics. It is instead a complicated—and sometimes contradictory—setting for advancing immigrant rights. Located in a conservative state, Democratic mayors and a mix of Democratic and Republican council members have governed the city of Houston since the early 1980s, with business interests—and a belief in small government—also important drivers of local policymaking. Advancing immigrant rights in Houston thus requires bipartisan support, which is not always easy to find, resulting in more centrist policies and initiatives than in more progressive immigrant gateway cities.

Given Houston's minimal public investments in immigrant programming, the city's assorted civil society organizations have shouldered a heavy burden in implementing federal immigration policies and pushing for local innovations in immigrant rights. Immigrant advocates in Houston cannot simply wage their campaigns by copying the playbooks of other cities such as Chicago, Los Angeles, and New York City, which boast relatively progressive Democratic city leadership and long-standing, powerful immigrant rights coalitions that are absent in Houston. Instead, immigrant rights advocacy in Houston requires an all-hands-on-deck approach that pulls together a wide range of disparate immigrant organizations, faith-based institutions, philanthropic organizations, labor unions, and business organizations. The remainder of this chapter examines just how Houston's demographic, political, and civic contexts have shaped this process.

Houston's Demographic Context

Immigration-Driven Population Diversity

Often described and celebrated as one of the nation's most diverse cities (e.g., Klineberg 2020a), Houston today is home to many recently arrived immigrants. However, the city's status as a key immigrant destination is not entirely new. As a major port city and energy industry hub, Houston attracted Italian and Jewish immigrants starting in the late nineteenth century through World War I, as well as a sizable number of Czechs before the Civil War. As was the case elsewhere in the United States, migration to Houston slowed with the imposition of the racist national origin quotas enacted as part of the federal Immigration Acts of 1921 and 1924, which barred immigrants from southern and eastern Europe and most of Asia. Houston would eventually become a major immigrant destination once again after World War II: while the enactment of the federal Immigration and Nationality Act of 1965 and the removal of national origin quotas facilitated economic and family-based migration from Latin America, Asia, and Africa, the federal Refugee Act of 1980 brought large numbers of refugees from these places to Houston.

Houston currently has about 662,000 foreign-born residents who make up a third of the city's population (ACS 2023a).[1] Between 2000 and 2014 alone, Houston gained over half a million foreign-born residents (Singer 2015), contributing to its population growth and demographic diversity. This diversity is a source of pride, and city officials like to point out that Houston hosts one of the biggest consular corps in the nation. This diversity, however, also poses a challenge for advancing a unified immigrant rights agenda that serves the needs and interests of all the city's immigrants. Houston now attracts newcomers from all over the world, including immigrants, refugees, and asylum seekers from Latin America, Asia, and Africa. They speak a staggering 145 different languages (Kriel 2015), which makes providing language access for them a key issue. The different circumstances of their arrival also create a need for a range of other immigrant-specific programs, including food and family assistance as well as physical and mental health supports.

Houston has long had, and continues to have, a large Latino immigrant population, and today, 69 percent of the city's foreign born hail from Latin America. Mexico (37 percent of all foreign born) is the top Latin American country of origin, followed by El Salvador (10 percent), Honduras (7 percent), and Guatemala (4 percent). Houston's geography partially explains why it is home to such a large Latin American immigrant population today. Mexicans, in particular, have a historic presence in the Southwest, which encompasses territory that once belonged to Mexico. Other historical push and pull factors are also at play, though. The Mexican Revolution of 1910–1920; the U.S.-sponsored civil wars in El Salvador, Guatemala, Honduras, and Nicaragua in the 1980s; and global recessions in the 1970s and 1990s all led Mexicans and Central Americans to leave their countries and settle in Houston as immigrants and refugees. The Bracero contract labor program (1942–1964) and the construction flurry that followed the 1970s oil boom also created many new employment opportunities in Houston that attracted immigrant workers—with or without papers—from south of the border (Jonas and Rodríguez 2021).

Immigrants from Asia make up Houston's second-largest immigrant group, composing 20 percent of all foreign-born individuals. Vietnam (4.3 percent of all foreign born) is the top country of origin in Asia, followed by India (3.6 percent) and China (2.9 percent). Many of Houston's Vietnamese came as refugees following the Vietnam War, while economic opportunities and family reunification have driven Indian and Chinese immigration. Compared with Latino immigrants, who are largely unified by the Spanish language (though increasing numbers speak indigenous languages), there is tremendous language and ethnic diversity among Houston's Asian immigrants. Many require English-language training as well as citizenship assistance, refugee resettlement services, cultural and religious resources, help in seeking employment and health care, and support for parents with children in local schools (Klineberg and Wu 2013). All told, Houston's immigrant population is hyperdiverse, defying a one-size-fits-all integration approach and requiring innovation from both city government officials and community advocates seeking to address their many and diverging needs and interests.

Bifurcated Socioeconomic Immigrant Realities

In addition to national origin and ethnoracial diversity, the human capital profiles of Houston immigrants reflect a spectrum of socioeconomic opportunities and challenges (see Table 1.1). Over a quarter (27 percent) of Hous-

TABLE 1.1 SELECTED CHARACTERISTICS OF HOUSTON'S FOREIGN-BORN POPULATION, 2017–2021

	Foreign Born
Population	662,251
Region of Birth	(%)
Europe	4.0
Asia	20.3
Africa	6.9
Oceania	0.3
Latin America	67.8
Northern America	0.8
Period of Entry	(%)
Entered 2010 or later	34.1
Entered 2000–2009	24.5
Entered before 2000	41.4
Citizenship	(%)
Naturalized U.S. citizen	32.9
Not a U.S. citizen	67.1
Ability to Speak English (5 yrs.+)	(%)
Speak only English at home	9.8
Speak language other than English at home	90.2
Speak English less than "very well"	59.7
Educational Attainment (25 yrs.+)	(%)
No high school degree	39.3
High school degree	19.7
Some college	14.2
Bachelor's degree	14.6
Graduate or professional degree	12.1
Occupation (16 yrs.+)	(%)
Management, business, science, arts	26.4
Service	24.0
Sales, office	12.0
Natural resources, construction, maintenance	21.9
Production, transportation, material moving	15.7
Earnings and Poverty Status in Past 12 Months	(%)
$1–$14,999	6.6
$15,000–$34,999	41.8
$35,000–$74,999	32.8
$75,000 and more	18.8
Below 100% of the federal poverty level	20.8
100% to 199% of the federal poverty level	27.1
Housing Tenure	(%)
Homeowner	38.7
Renter	61.3

Source: ACS 2023b.

ton's foreign born have a college degree or higher. These immigrants are part of a professional class with generally strong English-language skills, often working in Houston's emerging tech hub, premier medical centers, sprawling defense firms, and oil companies (ACS 2023b; Federal Reserve Bank of Dallas 2017). According to Houston's largest chamber of commerce, "big tech" is on the rise in Houston, as the city aims to attract workers—many of them immigrants—seeking a diverse but more affordable place to live and work than the expensive big tech cities on the East and West Coasts (GHP 2021; Texas CRES 2021). Additionally, immigrants own a quarter of the city's small businesses (CPPP 2017), many of which are part of the ethnic retail hubs and strip malls dotting the city.

Houston's immigrant population, however, is socioeconomically bifurcated. Alongside the many college-educated immigrants with well-paying jobs, 59 percent of immigrants in Houston have a high school degree or less and work in service sector jobs at the bottom of the postindustrial, hourglass economy (ACS 2023a; Understanding Houston 2023). Among the top ten service sector occupations for immigrants in Houston are maids and housecleaners, construction laborers, cooks, janitors, truck drivers, carpenters, ground maintenance workers, registered nurses, and cashiers. These jobs are highly precarious and generally offer few opportunities for upward mobility. They also tend to be nonunionized, especially in Texas, where "right to work" legislation and probusiness sentiment make union organizing—a top predictor of job quality—an uphill battle (Kalleberg 2011). In Houston, 2.9 percent of private sector workers are represented by a union, compared with 6.8 percent of all private sector workers in the United States. This disparity persists in the public sector: 18.3 percent of public sector workers in Houston are represented by a union, compared with 36.8 percent nationwide (Hirsch and Macpherson 2022). Many immigrants know economic hardship: half of all immigrants in Houston live at or below 200 percent of the federal poverty line, and many struggle to make ends meet.

Language limitations and precarious immigration status also cause significant numbers of Houston's immigrants to be economically precarious. Only 10 percent of immigrants in Houston speak only English, while 60 percent speak English less than "very well." More than two-thirds (67 percent) of Houston's immigrants are not U.S. citizens, and the Houston area is home to an estimated 506,000 undocumented immigrants, who qualify for little to no public assistance and have no legal work authorization (ACS 2023b; CPPP 2016; Capps and Soto 2018). Many refugees also live in precarious circumstances and face steep integration challenges, and despite Governor Abbott's withdrawal from official refugee resettlement efforts in 2020, Houston's diverse urban scene and thriving economy have long made it among the largest recipients of refugee arrivals in the country (Digilov and Sharim 2018; Kragie 2015). Finally, given its proximity to the U.S.-Mexico border and the robust migration industry that has developed in the city (Hernández-León 2008), Houston is often a first stop for clandestine border crossers fleeing violence and dire economic circumstances in their home countries, some placing themselves in the hands of nefarious human traffickers to make the journey. Few state and federal resources are available to address their plight, often leaving local governments and advocates scrambling to assist them.

Natural disasters and other emergencies have also had a disproportionate negative impact on Houston's immigrants, further compounding their precarity. After Hurricanes Ike (2008) and Harvey (2017) hit the Houston area, immigrants were more likely than native-born Houstonians to report job and income losses, even as they had access to fewer recovery resources to get back on their feet (Wu et al. 2018). The COVID-19 pandemic also hit Houston's low-wage immigrants particularly hard, leading local advocates to call for greater equity in resource distribution for health care, food, and housing, regardless of immigration and citizenship status (HILSC 2020c). These and other emergencies have threatened to crack the already fragile foundation on which many immigrant workers and their families in Houston stand.

Immigrant Dispersion and Suburban Sprawl

Houston's size, unprecedented sprawl, ongoing housing segregation, and poor public transit all complicate immigrant service provision. Houston ranks 4th in absolute population size but 43rd in terms of population density, with only 3,857 residents per square mile (Exner 2018). For such a large city, it has remarkably few zoning restrictions, and market-led land-use development strategies and vigorous annexations of peripheral areas have allowed Houston to swell to 667 square miles (Jargowsky 2002). This makes Houston the largest U.S. city by total land area, far larger than New York City (300 mi^2), Los Angeles (469 mi^2), and Chicago (227 mi^2). Houston's geographic spread has led to rapid suburban development, with residential areas abutting retail strip malls and neighborhoods divided and segregated by massive thruways that loop through this car-dependent city.

Houston's well-documented housing segregation (e.g., Levin 2015) has implications for coalition building across ethnoracial communities as well as for effective government and nonprofit service delivery. While affordable housing and the availability of jobs have drawn immigrants to Houston, wealth inequality and a legacy of discriminatory federal, state, and local housing policies have left Black and Latino city residents overrepresented in neighborhoods near industrial facilities, such as those near the port in southeast Houston, where environmental pollution and significant health problems abound (Douglas 2021; Trovall 2021). Moreover, gentrification threatens the city's historic Black neighborhoods, including the Third Ward, located just east of downtown, intensifying the challenge of securing affordable housing near the city center. Many Latino and Asian immigrants reside in the western and southwestern parts of the city, but they have increasingly shifted toward the city's east and north (and this is particularly true of the city's large Latino population) (Harden 2018). Yet the organizations that provide critical support services to immigrants are typically located downtown or in immigrant-dense, high-poverty neighborhoods like Gulfton in southwest Houston, making them unreachable for immigrants farther afield who do not have a car or cannot drive (de Graauw and Gleeson 2021b).

With massive freeways, cheap gas, and ample parking, Houston lacks an adequate public transit system that connects the different corners of the city with the larger metropolitan region to which many city residents have economic ties. Houston has no unified rail or metro system, and immigrants disproportionately rely on a limited public bus system that is considered unreliable and arduous (Hanna 2021). Despite a drop in ridership post-COVID (Delaughter 2022), the city's public bus and rail system—METRO, or the Metropolitan Transit Authority of Harris County—mostly services precarious Houston residents. These include many of the city's immigrants: 40 percent of bus riders have no vehicle to get them around the city and beyond (Air Alliance Houston 2021). Immigrants and other poor Houstonians also face other mobility challenges, including a lack of sidewalks, poor bikeability, and high traffic deaths (Haile 2019). Undocumented residents in Houston face additional structural barriers: ineligible for Texas driver's licenses and unable to drive legally, many also fear run-ins with local police and federal immigration officials (de Graauw and Gleeson 2021b). This makes basic activities like getting to school or work or seeking assistance from a government agency or community organization a major hassle for immigrants.

Houston's geographic sprawl presents more acute challenges for implementing programming and delivering services to immigrants than in denser immigrant cities with better public transit systems such as New York City, Chicago, Boston, and San Francisco. Houston's sprawl forces low-income families, including low-income immigrant families, to search for affordable housing farther and farther out from the city center (Bruegmann 2008). This trend has driven rapid growth in Houston's poor suburban neighborhoods and created new high-need immigrant suburban enclaves within city limits. These low-income and immigrant-dense suburbs receive far less attention from city officials, who focus on fighting poverty in inner-city areas (Martin 2017). Meanwhile, nongovernmental support organizations are often located far afield from Houston's immigrant-dense suburbs (de Graauw and Gleeson 2021b), limiting their usefulness.

Houston's Political Context

Despite Houston's clear need for policies and initiatives that support immigrants, its political context is unfavorable to designing, adopting, or implementing such policies. First, the city's political culture generally does not encourage local governments to take an activist role in promoting economic and social equity, including immigrant rights, instead preferring market-based solutions to address these issues (Vojnovic 2003). Second, the structure of Houston's government enables traditional city elites to control policymaking and provides few openings for immigrants and their advocates to mobilize and assert their voices. And third, deep-rooted partisan divisions between officials at different levels of government—especially around immigration issues—further stymie the advancement of immigrant rights in Houston.

The Archetypical Laissez-Faire City

Strong cultural beliefs in self-reliance and individualism characterize Houston's ethos of small government and low taxes, with scholars concluding that Houston is the archetypical "free enterprise," "capitalist," or "laissez-faire" city (Feagin 1988; Lamare 2000; Lin 1995). This approach did not stop Houston city officials from promoting ambitious local economic development projects—for example, by pursuing state and federal funding to develop its port, railways, highways, airports, oil and aerospace industries, and medical sector (Feagin 1988; Shelton 2017; Simpson 2019). Yet they have typically never embraced sustained government interventions to promote economic and social equity, especially not for poor Black and Hispanic residents (Vojnovic 2003). Houston has also not historically invested in immigrant rights initiatives, also due to lack of resources; despite a booming economy, the city has struggled with budget deficits due to the rising costs of the city's municipal pension system and caps on the city's power to tax residents and businesses (Fulton et al. 2020). Meanwhile, Texas state officials embrace a similarly minimalist government philosophy; Texas does not levy personal income taxes and, compared with other U.S. states, spends the least per capita on social services (Vojnovic 2003). This further hamstrings Texas localities, including Houston, from investing in pro-immigrant programming and development.

Traditional community power debates often pit elitists (e.g., Hunter 1953) against pluralists (e.g., Dahl 1961). Within this framework, Houston is best thought of as a hybrid where local elites continue to dominate the government structure even as a diversifying population increasingly residing outside Houston's urban core pushes for broader, more pluralist decision-making. During Houston's peak economic development years (1930s–1960s), a small group of politically active and powerful businesspeople known as the 8F Club (because of their regular gatherings in Suite 8F of the now demolished Lamar Hotel in downtown Houston) played key behind-the-scenes roles. These days are gone, but local business leaders still have a notable influence in Houston politics, often working with city officials in pursuit of economic success (Feagin 1988; Pratt 2004; Shelton 2017). As a result of the rapid diversification of Houston's population into the city's ever-growing suburban areas, a new generation of Black, Hispanic, and Asian civic leaders has emerged. These new actors have demanded a say in local decision-making on pressing economic, cultural, and political issues as diverse as pollution abatement, public education, historic preservation, transportation, and immigration (Pratt 2004; Shelton 2017).

This is a welcome trend for advancing immigrant rights. Indeed, studies on the local politics of immigrant rights underscore the importance of activist city officials with inclusive agendas and government structures that offer community members different ways to influence local decision-making (e.g., de Graauw 2021; de Graauw and Vermeulen 2016; Hayduk, Hackett, and Folla 2017). Yet Houston's laissez-faire political culture, characterized by a preference for promoting private economic needs over pluralist political participation, limits the potential for enacting and implementing policies that promote immigrant rights. Houston has a large geographic footprint, minimal public transportation connecting its sprawling suburbs to downtown, and no common public spaces suitable for staging mass protests (Binkovitz 2017). Taken together, this makes advancing immigrant rights more challenging in Houston than in places like New York City, Chicago, Boston, and San Francisco—all denser cities with extensive public transit systems, progressive and activist city officials, and a culture of civic participation (de Graauw 2021; de Graauw and Vermeulen 2016; Lauby 2019).

The Mayor and the City Council

Political power in Houston is concentrated in the mayor's office. Houston is a "home rule" city with a city charter, or city constitution, that outlines the organization, powers, and functions of city government. Houston's city charter establishes a strong mayor-council form of government with an executive mayor and a legislative city council separately elected by voters. This form of government is common in large U.S. cities, including New York City, Los Angeles, Chicago, and Philadelphia, but Houston stands out for having an especially strong mayor (Fulton 2020; Murray 1997). Specifically, the Houston mayor, who is popularly elected for a maximum of two consecutive four-year terms, has the power to prepare the city budget, implement and enforce city council legislation, appoint and remove department heads, and oversee municipal courts. The Houston mayor also presides over and votes during city council meetings. While the Houston mayor does not have veto power over the city council, this hardly diminishes the control of the mayor's office given that the mayor alone sets the council's weekly agenda (Fulton 2020). All said, mayoral support is critical for both the adoption and implementation of new legislation and initiatives, including those addressing immigrant rights.

Houston has had Democratic mayors since 1982. Despite key interventions, they have not consistently put immigrant rights at the top of their concerns, and their views on immigration are muted compared with mayors in more progressive cities. For example, though Lee Brown (1998–2004), Houston's first Black mayor, created the Office of Immigrant and Refugee Affairs in 2001 to enable the city to take a more active role in addressing immigrant issues, he staffed it with only one person (Rodrigues 2001). Later, after an undocumented immigrant shot and critically wounded a Houston police officer in 2009, Mayor Bill White (2004–2010) pursued Houston's participation in the federal 287(g) program to train local police and city jail personnel to assist U.S. Immigration and Customs Enforcement in apprehending and deporting undocumented immigrants, a move eventually opposed by the city council and community advocates (Olson and Carroll 2009b). Annise Parker (2010–2016), Houston's first openly gay mayor, collaborated with local organizations to encourage immigrants to apply for U.S. citizenship and President Obama's 2012 DACA program, though she consistently denied that Houston was a sanctuary city (DON 2015). More recently, Mayor Sylvester Turner (2016–2024), the city's second Black mayor, proclaimed in 2016 that Houston was a "Welcoming City" and, with philanthropic support, formed a multisector task force responsible for recommending city policies to promote immigrant integration (Welcoming Houston 2017). He too, though, has shied away from controversial issues such as sanctuary status protections and municipal ID cards for the city's many undocumented immigrants.

Houston's city council has the sole power to enact ordinances (i.e., local laws) and resolutions (i.e., statements of intent or proposed action), and it also approves the city's annual budget of more than $6 billion. Since 2011, the city council has had 16 popularly elected members who can serve up to two consecutive four-year terms: 11 members represent large districts of between 200,000 and 221,000 residents each (Districts A–K), and 5 are elected "at-large" to represent residents citywide (see Figure 1.1). Based on 2020 demographic data for the city's redistricting plan that will be effective in 2024, non-Hispanic White residents form the majority in one district and the plurality in two districts (Districts C, E, and G) and Hispanics form the majority of residents in four districts (A, H, I, and J). Black residents do not constitute the majority population in any district, but as a bloc, Black and Hispanic res-

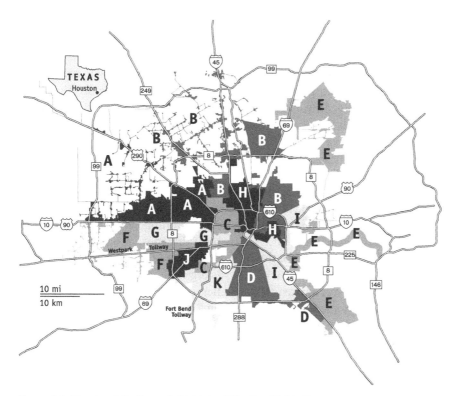

Figure 1.1 Houston City Council Districts, Effective 2024 *(Source: Mike Boruta, 2023)*

idents make up the majority in four districts (B, D, F, and K). Districts F, G, and C in southwest Houston have the highest concentrations of Asian residents, at 16, 12, and 11 percent, respectively, while all other districts have Asian populations of 8 percent or lower. Council members earn roughly $63,000 per year for what—per the city charter—is officially a part-time job, though representing the interests of these large and diverse districts in fact requires a full-time commitment (Monte 2019).

Between 1955 and 1979, Houston's city council consisted of 8 members, all elected at-large and all of whom were men (and most of whom were White). This system disadvantaged minority candidates, as it has in other cities with similar electoral arrangements (e.g., Engstrom and McDonald 1981; Trounstine and Valdini 2008), while the use of "white primaries" (in which only White people could vote), poll taxes, and complex voter registration laws had long excluded or diluted Black and Hispanic electoral influence in Houston politics (Murray 1997). Not surprisingly, then, Houston's city council rarely acted on minority community interests (Thomas and Murray 1986). After the 1965 federal Voting Rights Act (and its 1970 amendments) eventually compelled Houston in 1979 to expand its city council to 14 members, reorganized to include 9 members elected by district, council membership notably diversified.[2] In 1985, for example, the city council counted 4 Black officials, 1 Mexican American, and 2 women among its 14 members, who collectively were also notably younger than prior council members. This more pluralistic city council was not only more representative of the city's increasingly diverse population but also functioned as a counterweight to the powerful mayor (Thomas and Murray 1986).

The 16-member Houston city council elected in 2019 included 9 women and 6 Black officials. Other residents remained underrepresented between 2020 and 2024, with no Asian leaders on the city council and only 1 Hispanic in a city whose population at the time was 45 percent Hispanic (Jones 2019). This underrepresentation has implications for a range of issues that disproportionately impact Latinos and Asians, including immigration. In December 2022, the Houston chapter of the League of United Latin American Citizens (LULAC)—the oldest Hispanic civil rights organization in the United States—filed a federal lawsuit against the city, alleging that the city's five remaining at-large districts violate the federal Voting Rights Act and deprive Hispanics of the ability to elect representatives of their choice, resulting in council representation that does not adequately take account of the interests of the city's growing Hispanic population (Ura 2022). The last time a Hispanic was elected to one of Houston's five at-large districts was in 1999 (Jones 2019).[3] Houston stands apart from other large cities in how it elects its city council members; other major Texas cities, as well as other immigrant-dense cities such as New York City and Los Angeles, have all abandoned at-large district representation.

Underrepresentation on the Houston city council is a complex issue, and there are both supply- and demand-side explanations for it. For example, Houston council races are often uncontested and frequently do not include many Asian and Hispanic candidates. And while at-large races have tended to include more Hispanic candidates, success is unlikely because citywide campaigns are much costlier to run than district-level ones and because of lingering segregation in the city. Additionally, council elections are nonpartisan and held off cycle (i.e., not concurrent with presidential or midterm congressional elections). This has stymied turnout in Houston's municipal elections and skewed voter turnout, which is typically unrepresentative of a district's population (Lappie 2017). The resulting underrepresentation of immigrant populations does not bode well for the council's ability or willingness to pursue substantive policies that advance immigrant rights.

Indeed, Houston's city council has a mixed record on this front. It does not have a committee dedicated to immigrant issues like the New York City Council, but it does have an immigrant affairs office within the city's executive branch. Created in 2001 and currently named the Office of New Americans and Immigrant Communities, it seeks to facilitate the successful societal integration of immigrants. While it is important to have an office exclusively dedicated to diverse immigrant issues in a city with a foreign-born population of 662,000, its influence is limited given that it has only two staff members (de Graauw 2018). Houston also has a Mayor's Advisory Council of New Americans and a Mayor's Hispanic Advisory Board, both offering residents opportunities to provide input on the mayor's agenda on issues affecting the city's immigrant and Hispanic communities. Their ultimate impact, however, is unclear, and there are no comparable advisory councils for the city's large Black and growing Asian populations. Houston also lacks other standing advisory bodies dedicated to diversity issues, such as a human rights commission, which are common in other large cities. For a city of its size and diversity, Houston has relatively few government bodies dedicated to facilitating residents' civic participation, including on issues affecting immigrants.

Parties, Elections, and Partisanship

At the turn of the twentieth century, many large cities—including early gateways like New York City, Boston, Chicago, and San Francisco—were controlled by political machines, or local party organizations headed by "bosses" who dispensed jobs and assorted welfare benefits to residents in exchange for their loyalty in the voting booth (Reichley 1992). While these political machines were self-interested institutions that often pandered to immigrants who knew little about American political affairs, they also displayed significant grassroots organizational vigor and were important agents of immigrants' political integration and socioeconomic mobility (e.g., Allswang 1986). For better or worse, such machines never took hold in Houston, in large part because, unlike in cities on the East Coast and in the Midwest, there were relatively few European immigrants who could form a reliable voting bloc. Also, Houston's city government was relatively small, with few municipal jobs available for loyal immigrant voters and supporters. Finally, there was no meaningful party competition in Houston for most of the twentieth century, as the White-only Democratic Party put the Republican Party into the shadows between the 1890s and 1960s (Henthorn 2018; Key 1984; Murray 1997).

To this day, local party organizations are weak, with limited roles and influence in Houston politics. The city's many Democratic and Republican political clubs (which are affiliated with the Democratic and Republican Parties of Harris County, a large county of 4.7 million residents that includes nearly all of Houston's 2.3 million residents) have relatively little influence because municipal elections are nonpartisan (Lappie 2017; Murray 1997). Political clubs and parties do not nominate candidates for local political offices, and every local official is elected without a party label. Not only does this depress turnout in Houston city elections, but local party organizations also do not appear to be interested in using their limited resources and influence to engage immigrants around their interests. For instance, the party platforms as described on the websites of the Harris County Democratic and Republican Parties make no mention of diversity issues more broadly or immigrant issues more specifically. In short, local party organizations active in Houston have not been notable agents of immigrant integration in the past and are still not today.

While local elections in Houston are nonpartisan and local political parties are weak, local voters do have clear partisan leanings. While large U.S. cities tend to be Democratic strongholds (e.g., Thompson 2019), Houston remains notably split, with the balance of power often swaying between Republicans and Democrats. We can look at how residents of Harris County, which encompasses nearly all of Houston,[4] voted in recent presidential elections to get an impression of the partisan divisions in Houston (see Figure 1.2). While slightly larger percentages of Harris County voters supported Re-

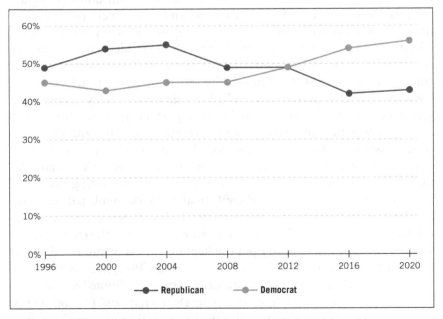

Figure 1.2 Partisan Leanings of Harris County Voters, 1996–2020
Note: Percentages of Harris County voters who voted for Republican and Democratic candidates in the general presidential elections between 1996 and 2020. (Data source: Harris County Election Division, Election Results Archive, https://www.harrisvotes.com/ElectionResults.)

publicans in the presidential elections between 1996 and 2008, they were evenly split in the 2012 presidential election. Slightly higher percentages of voters supported Democratic candidates in the 2016 and 2020 presidential elections. The Kinder Houston Area Survey, which has tracked the attitudes and beliefs of representative samples of Harris County residents for 40 years, notes that Houstonians have long been politically divided, though larger percentages of them indicate feeling aligned with the Democratic Party in recent years (Klineberg and Bozick 2021). In fact, Houston has become a political hotbed, with national politicians now looking to the city's and Harris County's competitive political environment as vital for flipping Texas from a Republican- to a Democratic-majority state (Livingston 2019).

Increasingly, the national Republican and Democratic Parties have different and polarized views on immigration issues. While Republicans tend to see immigration as a threat, want to reduce immigration, and support border and interior enforcement, most national Democrats have opposite views (Hammer and Kafura 2019). These national partisan divisions have solidified the substantial minority of Houston Republican voters who block local efforts to advance immigrant rights. However, as the city's population diversifies and the electorate becomes more Democratic, Houstonians' views are shifting in a more tolerant direction on a host of diversity issues (see Chapter 3 for more details). Recent Kinder Houston Area Surveys show that Houston residents of all races and ethnicities, including White people, are becoming more favorable toward different immigrant groups, including refugees, Muslims, and undocumented immigrants. More specifically, a growing number of Houstonians support policies that welcome refugees and create a pathway to citizenship for undocumented immigrants (Klineberg 2020b; Klineberg and Bozick 2021). This growing public support offers hope for future efforts in Houston to advance the rights of immigrants. This optimism depends, however, on the ability and willingness of the mayor and the city council to build support for inclusive policies and practices out of those increasingly tolerant public preferences.

Roughly a quarter-million foreign-born adult noncitizens are eligible to naturalize in Harris County (CSII 2016). They have the potential power to shift Houston's electorate toward more inclusive city policies affecting immigrant communities. Certain civic organizations are well aware of this potential electoral impact. In 2019, Houston's League of Women Voters attended each of the city's 16 naturalization ceremonies and registered more than 31,000 new citizens to vote (Mudd 2020). The trends are telling, especially for Hispanic voters, who constitute the largest immigrant and ethnic group in Houston. While eligible Hispanics still vote less frequently than Houston's general population, their turnout has grown in recent years: roughly 385,000 Hispanics voted in Houston during the 2016 elections, but around 531,000 did in 2020. And while some Hispanic voters have recently drifted rightward, over 80 percent of Hispanic voters in Houston supported the Democratic Party during the 2020 elections (Univision 2022). Growing numbers of Democratic Hispanic voters could pressure Houston city officials to enact more immigrant-inclusive policies. They could also motivate more Hispanics to run for local office, such as Robert Gallegos (the lone Hispanic on Houston's city council between 2020 and 2024), Gilbert Garcia (a bond investor and former chair of METRO), and Julian Martinez (a car dealer), who all joined Houston's crowded 2023 mayor's race (McGuinness 2023).

Houston's status as a home rule city offers both opportunities and challenges to enacting progressive policies. Houston's initiative process allows the city's registered voters to propose city charter amendments, ordinances, and recall petitions to remove elected and appointed city officials from office. This direct democracy process theoretically gives community members the chance to skirt the mayor and city council. It also has the potential to translate emerging tolerant opinions of Houston's diversifying population into new local laws. However, the city's voters have not used direct democracy to advance immigrant rights or other prodiversity policies. Even when they gathered enough signatures to be included on the ballot, progressive measures were defeated at the polls. In 1997, for example, 77 percent of voters rejected a ballot measure to raise Houston's hourly minimum wage from $4.75 to $6.50, which would have been a boon to low-wage immigrant workers (Langford 1997). Yet direct democracy has also been used to *reverse* the rare progressive policies adopted by the city council. This occurred in 2015 when opponents of the Houston Equal Rights Ordinance used the referendum process to overturn a law banning housing and workplace discrimination based on sexual orientation and gender identity. In sum, Houston's home rule processes have not been effective tools for advancing immigrant rights as in some other cities with direct democracy, notably San Francisco (de Graauw 2016).

Houston in a Multilevel Governmental Perspective

Houston must be understood in the context of the federal, state, and larger metropolitan political settings in which it is embedded (e.g., de Graauw and Gleeson 2021b). In the U.S. federal system, cities are hierarchically subordinate both to their states and the federal government, which courts have ruled has exclusive power over immigration and citizenship issues (Rodríguez 2017). Given that both the federal government and the state of Texas have focused on anti-immigrant, enforcement-only policies and practices, the U.S. federal system creates notable constraints for Houston city officials and community advocates with pro-immigrant agendas (e.g., de Graauw 2021). Houston officials, however, also take cues from nearby municipal jurisdictions, including counties, many of which are largely anti-immigrant as well. This also heightens the importance of the larger metropolitan context for how Houston city officials address immigrant rights (e.g., de Wilde and Nicholls 2021).

At the federal level, despite differences in rhetoric and resources devoted to immigration control, the administrations of Presidents Obama (Democrat), Trump (Republican), and Biden (Democrat) have all focused on immigration enforcement. Obama, dubbed the "deporter-in-chief" by immigrant rights advocates, deported three million people while in office, more than any other president before or after him (Guerrero 2021). While Trump prioritized *all* undocumented immigrants for removal, Biden did not fundamentally shift focus, though he did limit enforcement actions to certain immigrants in certain locations (Chishti and Bolter 2022). There has also been long-standing gridlock in Congress over potential reforms that would benefit the country's estimated 11 million undocumented immigrants, with little attention paid to the role that the federal government can play in funding and coordinating immigrant integration. All said, the enforcement-centered national policy landscape sends clear cues to Houston city officials that the promotion of immigrant rights is not a priority.

Texas state officials, who are overwhelmingly Republican, add a notably conservative layer to Houston's political landscape. Remarkably, Texas state officials—including then governor and two-time Republican presidential candidate Rick Perry—pioneered the Texas Dream Act (HB1403 in 2001 and SB1528 in 2005), allowing eligible undocumented students to receive in-state tuition rates and state financial aid at public universities and community colleges. Yet as the national Republican Party has moved to the right in subsequent decades, Republican state lawmakers have attacked these and other landmark policies. In 2014 and 2018, state officials led multistate lawsuits against President Obama's immigration initiatives, culminating in the effective rescission of the 2012 DACA program benefitting undocumented youth. In 2017, Texas legislators enacted SB4, a law that resembles Arizona's controversial 2010 "show me your papers" legislation (SB1070) and effectively bans sanctuary cities in the state. In 2020, Republican governor Greg Abbott notified the Trump administration that Texas would not be resettling any refugees in the coming fiscal year, and in 2022 and 2023, he deployed the National Guard to the U.S.-Mexico border and had floating wall border buoys installed in the Rio Grande to block immigrants from entering Texas and the United States.

Houston's metropolitan political context does not encourage inclusive city policies and practices around immigrant rights either. Almost all of the city of Houston is located in Harris County, Texas's largest and the nation's third-largest county with a diverse population of 4.7 million. While the majority of Harris County voters supported Republicans in all but one presidential election between 1952 and 2008, its growing Hispanic population has helped turn the county blue since the 2008 presidential election that brought Barack Obama to the White House (Ura 2016). However, the other 12 counties that make up the larger Houston metropolitan region include many staunchly conservative suburban and rural counties, whose elected officials favor enforcement over integration approaches. Notably, following pressure from local immigrant rights advocates, Harris County ended its 287(g) agreement with U.S. Immigration and Customs Enforcement in 2017, but six suburban and rural counties surrounding Houston (i.e., Chambers, Galveston, Matagorda, Montgomery, Waller, and Wharton) did enter into such agreements (ICE 2023). These 287(g) agreements allowed participating counties to partner with the federal government's enforcement apparatus to find and deport undocumented immigrants.

To visualize how the U.S. federal system divides and shares powers between the federal government, the states, and local governments, scholars often invoke images of a layer or marble cake (e.g., Grodzins 1960). *Layer cake* (or dual) federalism refers to a political arrangement where power is divided between the federal and lower levels of government and where each government level has clearly defined roles and operates in its own separate sphere. With *marble cake* (or cooperative) federalism, different levels of government instead share power, collaborate on policy, and have interrelated policy goals and administrative duties. The latter is more helpful for understanding how Houston city officials have interacted with other local as well as state and federal officials on immigration issues. Houston city officials, however, have different immigration policy goals and have been more supportive of promoting immigrant rights and immigrant integration compared with other local, state, and federal officials. As a result, intergovernmental relations can be strained, with less flexible and less effective policy cooperation than suggested by the marble cake type of federalism.

Houston's Civic Context

Rarely do the actions of government officials alone advance immigrant rights. Local progress often requires the ongoing advocacy of civil society organizations that serve and represent immigrants, including immigrant organizations, faith-based institutions, philanthropic organizations, labor unions, and business organizations (e.g., de Graauw and Bloemraad 2017). In Houston, civil society organizations have indeed been active on assorted immigrant issues, including language access, labor rights, education, refugee resettlement, and access to immigration legal services (e.g., de Graauw and Gleeson 2021b; Digilov and Sharim 2018; Gleeson 2012; Hagan and Baker 1993; HILSC 2015). Especially in the absence of activist Houston city officials, these civil society organizations have been important agents of change for immigrant rights.

Compared with other big gateway cities, however, Houston has a sparser infrastructure of civil society organizations, including those serving immigrants. In 2018, there were 5 registered nonprofit organizations per 10,000 residents in the larger Houston metropolitan area, compared with 9.8 in metropolitan New York, 7.4 in metropolitan Los Angeles, and 8.5 in metropolitan Chicago (Maciag 2019). Additionally, organizational differences in interests, resources, and constraints have made coalition building difficult, and while civil society organizations in Houston do work together, no overarching immigrant rights advocacy coalition has a significant influence in local politics. In contrast, the New York Immigration Coalition in New York City, the Coalition for Humane Immigrant Rights in Los Angeles, and the Illinois Coalition for Immigrant and Refugee Rights in Chicago are long-standing immigrant rights coalitions—all dating from the 1980s—with notable clout in local political affairs.

In the absence of a larger immigrant rights advocacy coalition, the promotion of immigrant rights in Houston has necessitated an all-hands-on-deck, issue-by-issue approach, with organizations at times strategically allying with strange bedfellows in narrowly framed advocacy campaigns, a phenomenon discussed more fully in Chapter 2. The remainder of this chapter discusses four key subsets of Houston's immigrant-facing civil society sector, highlighting the varied motivations, resources, and constraints these organizations confront when seeking to advance immigrant rights.

Immigrant Organizations and Faith-Based Institutions

Houston is home to a growing number of immigrant organizations (including worker centers) and faith-based institutions that provide services to immigrants and advocate on their behalf to the city government and beyond. Notable immigrant organizations that focus on advocacy include the *Fe y Justicia* (Faith and Justice) Worker Center, *Familias Inmigrantes y Estudiantes en la Lucha* (FIEL, Immigrant Families and Students in the Struggle), Boat People SOS, the Organization of Chinese Americans (OCA)–Greater Houston, the Central American Resource Center (CRECEN), and the local United We Dream affiliate. Also active are several large faith-based organizations that offer critical social and legal services to immigrants, including Catholic Charities, YMCA International Services, Justice for Our Neighbors, and Memorial Assistance Ministries. Most of these organizations operate in immigrant-dense neighborhoods in southwest Houston or near the city center. Some organizations have been around for several decades (e.g., Boat People

SOS and CRECEN, both created in the 1980s), but others opened their doors more recently (e.g., FIEL and United We Dream, created in 2007 and 2008, respectively). Most organizations were established as a response to an immigration crisis, whether responding to large refugee flows from Asia and Central America or addressing the plight of the city's large undocumented population.

These organizations have varied interests. While some serve all immigrants in Houston, others focus on addressing the issues and concerns of specific immigrant nationality groups (e.g., Mexicans), pan-ethnic groups (e.g., Latinos), or immigrant categories (e.g., undocumented immigrants, refugees, unaccompanied minors). They may focus on specific immigrant concerns, such as workplace rights, while others address a wider range of issues including education, housing, health care, interactions with local law enforcement, and access to immigration legal services. Whatever their focus—and regardless of whether they advocate policies or provide services or both—immigrant organizations and faith-based institutions bring their crucial grassroots community expertise to debates about immigrant rights in Houston (see Chapter 2 for examples). Most organizations are not local chapters of national organizations, and they operate primarily in the Houston neighborhoods where immigrants live. They fill a number of gaps left by sparse government services, typically providing services and information in linguistically accessible and culturally appropriate ways. In turn, they have been able to develop an unrivaled expertise on Houston's diverse immigrant communities, which has helped them identify advocacy agendas critical to advancing immigrant rights.

It has been a struggle, though, to translate this hard-earned community expertise and trust into tangible influence with Houston city officials on immigrant rights policies. These organizations tend to lack the resources traditionally associated with political influence, including making campaign contributions or delivering votes. They run on tight budgets and have limited resources to invest in advocacy, such as paid staff positions exclusively dedicated to immigrant rights advocacy or get-out-the-vote campaigns. They also have difficulty delivering voters because many of their clients and members lack citizenship or even legal status. Most are also 501(c)(3) not-for-profit organizations, which are subject to government restrictions on the amount and types of advocacy they can do. Their tax-exempt status shields them from paying federal income tax and allows their donors to deduct their contributions, but only a small part of their activities can involve lobbying, and they are totally barred from partisan electoral activities (de Graauw 2016). Given these constraints, Houston's immigrant organizations and faith-based institutions cannot secure local immigrant rights victories on their own.

Philanthropic Organizations

The city's market-oriented approach to governance has long meant that Houston must rely on charitable endeavors to meet certain needs. The economic elite, whose progrowth policies drove Houston from a small mercantile city in the second half of the nineteenth century to become a Sun Belt metropolis after World War II, has historically been responsible for the philanthropic undertakings in the city. Early in the twentieth century, a handful of benevolent entrepreneurs promoted ad hoc charity projects to address the growing economic disparity and social challenges accompanying Houston's rapid urbanization and industrialization (Pratt 2004). Over time, however, the city's philanthropic community became more institutionalized, notably through large trusts and smaller private foundations set up by entrepreneurs who had made fortunes in lumber, cattle, construction and real estate, and the oil and energy industry (Henthorn 2018; Pratt 2004). According to data from the National Center for Charitable Statistics, Harris County was home to about 1,200 foundations in 2020. The priorities of these philanthropies have focused on funding nonprofit social services and building up medical facilities (e.g., the Texas Medical Center), the arts (e.g., the Houston Symphony, the Museum of Fine Arts, the Houston Ballet), and higher education institutions (e.g., Rice University, University of Houston) (Henthorn 2018; Pratt 2004).

At the beginning of the twentieth century, Houston's philanthropic sector largely focused on assisting poor White residents. The more disadvantaged poor Black and Hispanic Houstonians received little from elite giving, forcing them to rely on self-help for social uplift through ethnic churches and fraternities (Henthorn 2018). Today, Houston has a diverse ecosystem of philanthropic organizations, including several focused on newer immigrant communities. Notably, in 2013, the Houston Endowment (a large private foundation established in 1937 by Jesse Jones, a member of the 8F Club) and the Simmons Foundation (a small private foundation created in 1993 and now focused on building power in marginalized communities) spearheaded the formation of the Houston Immigration Legal Services Collaborative. Bringing together nonprofit immigration legal services providers from across metropolitan Houston, the Houston Immigration Legal Services Collaborative is a funder-driven collaborative that seeks to increase legal services capacity and improve the ability of low-income immigrants to access holistic immigration legal services, including assistance in applying for deferred action and citizenship as well as in fighting deportation and securing asylum status.

Increased funding for immigration legal services notwithstanding, philanthropic organizations in Houston have not historically played key roles in advocating for local immigrant rights. Many philanthropic organizations are averse to funding policy advocacy activities, whether by choice or because they are discouraged by the substantial taxes they would have to pay over lobbying expenditures. Instead, they focus on giving grants to 501(c)(3) nonprofits that provide services to local residents. And while a few foundations, notably the Houston Endowment and the Simmons Foundation, specifically focus their grant making on immigrant communities or immigrant issues, most local foundations do not. Instead, they address pressing human needs such as food security, housing, education, and health care. Though these foundation-funded services undoubtedly also benefit immigrants, our data suggest that they might not be meeting or identifying immigrant-specific needs.

Labor Unions

Labor unions are often at the forefront of immigrant rights advocacy in Houston today. The Harris County AFL-CIO, long the major union federation in Houston, was reconfigured in 2015 into the Texas Gulf Coast Area Labor Federation of the American Federation of Labor–Congress of Industrial Organizations (AFL-CIO). When the national Change to Win Coalition broke away from the AFL-CIO in 2005, they took several immigrant-focused unions with them, including SEIU (Service Employees International Union), UNITE-HERE! (the Union of Needletrades, Industrial, and Textile Employees–Hotel Employees and Restaurant Employees Union, which merged in 2004), UFCW (United Food and Commercial Workers), and several construction unions. Some locals have reaffiliated with the AFL-CIO, though there is still a split within the larger national labor movement. In Houston, union locals have continued to work in solidarity, especially around issues of immigration and immigrant justice. Today, UNITE-HERE! Local 23 represents workers across a dozen states, including those employed at Houston's airports and several downtown hotels; SEIU Texas organizes security guards, janitors, and healthcare workers in the city; and the Houston Gulf Coast Building and Construction Trades Council encompasses several construction unions. All these unions have seen a rise in their immigrant workforce in recent years (Gleeson 2012).

Immigration poses at least three opportunities for unions in Houston. First, an overwhelming number of low-wage workers in Houston today are foreign born, as already noted. This worker demography has prompted unions to organize both old and new waves of immigrant workers as a matter of necessity and organizational survival. Second, unions in Houston have become key actors in local immigration politics. They often organize delegations to city council meetings and gather petition signatures, and labor leaders have served on local government advisory councils dedicated to immigrant issues, advocating for various wage policies to address the needs of the city's precarious immigrant workforce. And third, immigrant rights have become an important platform for coalition building and solidarity with immigrant communities that have been desperately needed allies for unions during their assorted campaigns. As such, Houston unions have been at the forefront of many immigrant rights mobilizations in recent years. For example, the 2003 Immigrant Workers Freedom Ride rolled through Houston with many labor leaders on board. Rank-and-file union members have also filled the streets during the many May 1 immigrant rights marches, especially following the 2005 congressional efforts to further criminalize immigrants.

Despite their strong and growing interest in immigrant issues, unions in Houston have fewer resources to organize and serve immigrants than those in other large cities with more powerful labor movements, such as New York City, Los Angeles, and Chicago. According to 2021 metropolitan area data, Houston has relatively low unionization levels: 1.8 percent of private sector workers are union members in metropolitan Houston, compared to 6.1 percent nationwide. There are an estimated 48,000 private sector union members in the larger Houston metropolitan area, compared with 851,000 in metropolitan New York, 420,000 in metropolitan Los Angeles, and 340,000 in metropolitan Chicago (Hirsch and Macpherson 2022). Fewer members mean unions have fewer resources to advance their priorities, including supporting immigrant rights. Texas's "right to work" policies further compound the resource constraints of Houston labor unions by not requiring all represented workers to become dues-paying members.[5] As a result, union organizers in Houston typically must spread their scarce resources thinly across several cities or even across several states, all the while confronting employers whose fierce union-busting strategies often enjoy public support. While Houston unions have gained substantial legitimacy in some circles of city politics, they still have far fewer political allies, even among Democrats, than local business organizations.

Despite their low membership levels and scant resources, Houston unions are formidable advocates for immigrant rights and have achieved some notable immigrant rights victories, often with immigrants of color leading the campaigns. Unions have strategically negotiated these constraints to forge diverse, sometimes unexpected collaborations. Houston union locals belong to federated organizations tied to state, national, and international unions. Leveraging these connections, many have taken a regional focus extending beyond the city to a broader swath of the Gulf Coast (Reynolds 2017). This shift has allowed member unions to reach workers of color and advocate for immigrants more effectively (AFL-CIO 2013), in part by drawing on a broader base of members, pooling resources, and allying with regional and statewide efforts. This is reflected in both the consolidation of the regional Texas

Gulf Coast Area Labor Federation AFL-CIO and the statewide membership of many union locals in Houston, including SEIU Texas, whose tagline is "Stronger Together."

Another strategy has been to collaborate with, and sometimes help incubate, nonunion worker centers, such as the *Fe y Justicia* Worker Center (created in 2006 with support from the national Interfaith Worker Alliance and the local AFL-CIO council), the Workers Defense Project (which began in Austin in 2002 and later expanded to Dallas and Houston), and several day labor centers that once operated with support from the Houston mayor's office. Drawing on a wide base of public support, these nonunion labor organizations have become essential allies to union campaigns in an era of union decline, pushing employers to comply with basic labor standards, such as through the famed Justice Bus, which often publicly shamed nefarious employers who refused to pay their workers. Finally, Houston unions have strategically collaborated with high-profile business organizations that at times articulate religious or business arguments to advance immigration reforms.

Business Organizations

Compared to labor organizations, business organizations have amassed significant political power, forming a pillar of Houston's conservative political structure. Prime among them is the Greater Houston Partnership (GHP), which represents more than 1,000 businesses in metropolitan Houston and was formed in 1989 from the merger of the Greater Houston Chamber of Commerce, the Houston Economic Development Council, and the Houston World Trade Association. The GHP has commissioned reports, convened a taskforce on immigration, and participated in public discussions about local political matters. Several high-profile Houston business leaders, including construction magnate Stan Marek, have long spoken out on immigration matters. Marek has advocated for the repeal of employer sanctions for hiring undocumented workers and in favor of a "sensible" immigration reform he has dubbed "ID and Tax." Marek has testified before city, state, and federal officials and regularly shares his views on assorted immigration issues in op-eds in local newspapers (e.g., Marek 2015, 2016, 2022). Prominent immigration lawyers such as Charles Foster and Gordon Quan—of Foster LLP and Quan Law Group PLLC law firms—have captured a sizable share of Houston's immigration services market. Foster and Quan have also become important voices for national immigration reform and local welcoming policies.

Houston's ethnic business associations play an important role not only in reviving the city's urban core while promoting cultural preservation in local ethnic neighborhoods (Knapp and Vojnovic 2016) but also in local immigration debates. Most prominently, Houston's Hispanic Chamber of Commerce has sponsored efforts to connect immigrants with assorted legal and social services, including assistance with family separation, deferred action for undocumented youth, and COVID-related issues (HHCC 2022). Houston's Asian Chamber of Commerce, meanwhile, has worked alongside pan-Asian social justice organizations such as OCA–Greater Houston in an expansive approach to promote civil rights. Smaller business associations have emerged to advocate for immigrant entrepreneurs and local retail districts like Chinatown, the southwestern city district hit hard by COVID and the subsequent worsening of anti-Asian sentiment and violence.

On the whole, few of Houston's business organizations actively support progressive approaches to immigration and immigrant rights, instead preferring middle-of-the-road positions. This is unsurprising given the market-based solutions that businesses everywhere typically promote. Houston's business organizations are united by a desire to boost economic development and reduce regulatory burdens on business owners. Their concerns include reducing the threat of federal immigration audits and ensuring a continued flow of immigrant labor to fuel the city's business engines, and this at times results in advocacy agendas that overlap with the pro-immigrant positions of immigrant rights organizations. Businesses articulate these interests alongside a parallel push for continued open global trade, as evidenced by the GHP's Business Beyond Borders program and its engagement with Houston's robust consular infrastructure. With over 90 nations staffing consular offices, Houston boasts the third-largest consular corps in the nation after New York City and Los Angeles. Furthermore, many area companies and associations such as the Greater Houston Restaurant Association have also vocally defended the Obama-era DACA program to retain local employees and consumers (Stewart 2021).

Houston business organizations have far more resources with which to voice their advocacy demands than do resource-strapped community organizations. In 2008, the GHP formed Americans for Immigration Reform, pledging $12 million for a media campaign to back federal immigration reform. Many Houston business leaders, including Stan Marek and Texans for Sensible Immigration Policy founder (and self-avowed Republican and Donald Trump supporter) Norman Adams, have deep roots in local faith communities, and they rely on both economic arguments and religious moral suasion in political debates about immigration issues. Marek even published a book highlighting the business case for rejecting employer sanctions against hiring undocumented workers based on his own experiences in running a large construction business in Houston (Steffy and Marek 2021). At the same time, even Houston's most powerful business leaders face an uphill battle in advancing pro-immigrant policies. While they have collaborated with local labor leaders, these uneasy alliances have fissured quickly when labor organizing campaigns focused on improving immigrant worker rights. National and Texas Republican politics also hem in Houston business organizations. While most Houston business leaders are political conservatives, they do not always see eye to eye with Republican governor Greg Abbott on immigration issues. Abbott has famously led the legal fight to end DACA, advocated the hypermilitarization of Texas's southern border, and closed Texas to the resettlement of new refugees. The business case for immigrant rights undoubtedly remains compelling in Houston but is difficult to sell elsewhere in restrictionist Texas.

Conclusion

The Houston case helps us understand how a city's demographic, political, and civic contexts shape the ways actors seek to advance immigrant rights at the local level. The next chapter presents four recent case studies of immigrant rights advocacy in Houston to illustrate how governmental and nongovernmental actors have worked with each other, in both collaborative and confrontational ways, to navigate this challenging context: (1) the 2001 creation and precarious institutionalization of a city immigrant affairs office; (2) responses by the Houston Police Department and the Harris County Sheriff's Office to federal immigration enforcement efforts; (3) local public-private partnerships aimed at increasing access to federal immigration benefits and relief, such as U.S. citizenship and the 2012 DACA program; and (4) the strange bedfellow coalitions involving labor, immigrant rights, faith, and business leaders who were critical to a successful 2013 campaign to combat wage theft.

2

Between Sanctuary and Enforcement

The Politics of Immigrant Rights in Houston

While Houston is a demographically diverse city reflecting earlier and contemporary waves of immigrants, it remains a bastion of conservative state and federal representatives, even though local levels of partisanship have gradually shifted to the left. This political atmosphere and the notable influence of business interests on city politics have required community organizations and other advocates to be strategic about how they respond to the needs and interests of immigrants. Many other studies have explored immigrant advocacy in overall progressive cities such as New York City, Los Angeles, and Chicago, but Houston presents a useful case for understanding how local advocates navigate an environment that is often hostile to immigrant rights. *What do local immigrant rights battles look like in Houston? And how did local advocates eventually make progress?*

This book illustrates how diverse governmental and nongovernmental actors have worked with and against each other to navigate Houston's challenging context. We focus on four institutional sites: (1) the Houston immigrant affairs office, created in 2001; (2) the Houston Police Department and the Harris County Sheriff's Office, and their responses to federal immigration enforcement efforts; (3) local partnerships between city officials and local civil society organizations to help immigrants access federal immigration benefits and relief; and (4) the strategic collaborations among labor, immigrant rights, faith, and business leaders that led to a successful 2013 campaign to combat wage theft.

The Creation and Institutionalization of Houston's Immigrant Affairs Office

After Congress failed to enact comprehensive federal immigration reform in 2006–2007, many U.S. cities (and states) created offices to promote immigrant integration. There are over 40 such immigrant affairs offices in the United States today, and all large cities—including New York City, Los Angeles, Chicago, and Philadelphia—have engaged in this type of immigrant-focused municipal institution building (de Graauw 2018). Houston created its office in 2001, one of the first in the country, and it initially was quite vocal about supporting all immigrants, including the undocumented. While the office has provided valuable immigrant services and advocacy, often in collaboration with immigrant organizations and the city's business elite, it has faced notable challenges, with Houston's conservative and business-dominated political context preventing it from doing more.

In 2001, Mayor Lee Brown issued an executive order creating the Mayor's Office of Immigrant and Refugee Affairs (MOIRA). Brown, a former New York City Police Department commissioner and Houston's first Black mayor, elected in 1997, recognized Houston's demographic and electoral reality. The city had a growing population of Latino immigrants who needed city resources and would one day become potential voters. "Because of the large Hispanic population," Brown explained, "I formed the Hispanic Advisory Committee, with representative leaders in the Hispanic community."[1] This committee, which predated MOIRA, met monthly to inform Mayor Brown of the issues confronting Latino immigrants. One issue that "kept cropping up," he said, "was access to services, particularly city services."[2] Committee members lobbied Brown to create an office to address these service issues. Gordon Quan, a Chinese American immigration lawyer and a Democrat elected to an at-large city council seat in 1999, was an early advocate of a city-run immigrant affairs office. He explained that "nobody on city council cared about the issue" at a time when the council was focused on "government consolidation and budget cutbacks, not creating a new office."[3] Recognizing the demand but lacking widespread city council support (even among the three Hispanics on the city council at the time), Brown created the office unilaterally by executive order.

Since political power in Houston is concentrated within the mayor's office, this aided the creation of this initiative. Mayor Brown explained that he strategically "put [MOIRA] in the Office of the Mayor, so it can carry with it the prestige of the mayor's office," adding that it would be "politically unwise for a council member to oppose this."[4] Brown funded one full-time person to staff the office, choosing Benito Juárez, an immigrant from Guatemala who he described as someone who "knows the Hispanic community, has the respect of the community."⁵ Juárez had long worked as an activist in Central American community organizations and the United Food and Commercial Workers union. Alongside MOIRA, Brown also created the Mayor's Advisory Council on Immigrant and Refugee Affairs (MACIRA), a volunteer body that met every two months to advise him on assorted immigrant issues in Houston. The mayor chose a diverse and high-powered group of people as members of MACIRA, including, as one staff recalled, "immigration attorneys, small business representatives, the head of the AFL-CIO, and representatives from local churches, HISD [the Houston Independent School District], and immigrant rights organizations."⁶ Brown himself attended many MACIRA meetings, granting members direct access to him and opportunities to influence his agenda and policies.

According to Brown, MOIRA's role was "to represent the mayor in helping immigrants in the city." Serving undocumented immigrants was the office's central goal, as laid out in its initial mission statement: "The policy of MOIRA is to encourage access by all persons residing in the city of Houston, regardless of nation of birth or current citizenship status, to the full benefits, opportunities, and services that are provided and administered by the city of Houston" (Carroll and Olson 2009). In 2003, MOIRA published a comprehensive resource guide with information about government, immigration, health, and housing services, as well as a guide for both contractors and day laborers outlining workers' rights and employers' responsibilities—a major issue for which advocates had demanded support. Office staff also logged workers' complaints, notably instances of wage theft commonly experienced by undocumented workers (Pinkerton 2007). These issues were highlighted in MOIRA's monthly email newsletters, which were sent to community, government, business, and ethnic media partners.

During the 2001 election season, Republican city council members attacked MOIRA's inclusive mission and questioned Brown's mayoral record. Orlando Sanchez, a conservative Cuban immigrant elected to an at-large council seat between 1996 and 2002, was running for mayor against the two-time Democratic incumbent Brown and campaigned on public safety concerns, including immigration issues. He argued that MOIRA made poor use of city funding during times of fiscal stress and that the office attracted undocumented immigrants to Houston. "When they first started, [MOIRA] had a mission statement that was sort of promoting illegal immigration," Sanchez explained when recalling his opposition.⁷ "And I thought, I'll be damned. We're taking tax dollars now, and we got this mayor and this leftist militant guy, Benito Juárez . . . tapping into city resources to build a coalition of illegal aliens to even promote more. I thought that was inappropriate."⁸ Other conservative council members attacked MOIRA along similar lines, advocating for small government and fiscal prudence. Sanchez won 40 percent of the first round of mayoral voting (against Brown's 43 percent) and then narrowly lost to Brown in a run-off election (Associated Press 2001). With Brown victorious, MOIRA remained safely ensconced inside the Office of the Mayor through his final term as mayor.

Sanchez renewed his attacks on MOIRA in 2003 when he ran again for mayor, a race he lost this time to Bill White, a moderate Democrat with strong ties to the business community (Williams 2003). White maintained support for MOIRA but moved it under the Citizens Assistance Office, a mayoral office focused on constituent services. MOIRA had several successes under Mayor White, including the development of a partnership with local nonprofits and immigration lawyers to offer monthly Citizenship and Immigration Forums to help legal immigrants to naturalize (see subsequent discussion). However, between 2006 and 2009, three incidents involving undocumented immigrants who killed or critically wounded Houston police officers shifted public opinion and shone a new critical light on the office and the mayor (Carroll and Lee 2009; Grant and Mack 2006; Pinkerton 2009b).

These rare tragedies fueled criticism of Houston's unofficial status as a sanctuary city and intensified attacks on MOIRA. Responding to this pressure, Mayor White directed the Houston Police Department to join the controversial Secure Communities immigration enforcement program in late 2009 (as detailed subsequently). As controversy loomed, Houston's city council cut municipal funding for MOIRA's work with immigrant day laborers. Furthermore, when it came time for the city to renew a $100,000 federally funded contract with a local day labor center, six Republican members on the city council opposed it. Though this day labor center helped undocumented immigrants find work and address labor abuses, critics on the city council argued that supporting its work would encourage undocumented immigration (*Houston Chronicle* 2006). While the contract was eventually approved, the controversy caused "unprecedented sensitivity toward MOIRA," according to MOIRA internal records, making its work and collaborations with day labor centers much more challenging to carry forward.

MOIRA struggled to survive during White's final years as mayor (2008–2009). To deflect the city council's constant attacks, MACIRA recommended that the mayor purge any reference to undocumented immigrants from MOIRA's mission. The new mission statement, adopted in 2009, subsequently read, "MOIRA's mission is to encourage good citizenship and facilitate integration of immigrant and refugee communities living in the city. This includes educating immigrant communities about their rights and responsibilities, as well as services provided and administered by the city of Houston" (Carroll and Olson 2009). As MOIRA was now neutral on its support for undocumented immigrants, its critics on the city council had a harder time characterizing Houston as a sanctuary city.

Facing mayoral term limits, White was preparing for his 2010 gubernatorial run against Republican incumbent Rick Perry by toughening his stance on immigration enforcement to appeal to Texas's conservative voters. Immigration was a racially charged priority issue among Texans, the majority of whom trended conservative on the issue. Indeed, in a 2010 University of Texas poll, 65 percent of respondents supported the adoption of an Arizona-style immigration law, which would allow police to "ask about the immigration status of anyone they stop for any reason" (Ramsey 2010). White subsequently "distanced himself from MOIRA and stopped attending MACIRA meetings," and he forbade MOIRA from seeking external funding to support its programs, foreclosing the possibility that the program would grow.[9] White also moved Benito Juárez, MOIRA's sole staff person throughout his administration, out of city hall to a branch office of the city's health department in southwest Houston. "He was sort of put away, isolated, put on the back burner," one city official commented.[10] While this move placed Juárez closer to the immigrant communities MOIRA aimed to serve, it removed him from interacting daily with others in Houston's power center.[11]

Annise Parker succeeded White as mayor from 2010 to 2016. A Democrat and Houston's first openly gay mayor, Parker sought to strengthen and destigmatize MOIRA by reorganizing and renaming it. Benito Juárez stayed on as manager, and Parker added Terence O'Neill, who had worked for Parker when she was a city council member and then city controller, as MOIRA director. Parker also placed the office within the Department of Neighborhoods, a new department created in 2011 to enhance efficiency by consolidating six city offices focused on reducing blight and making neighborhoods cleaner and safer. This reorganization elevated MOIRA in the Houston bureaucracy, put it on stronger institutional footing, and better insulated it from city officials who wished to shut it down. The office now had a small budget to support its work. "It wasn't a lot, about $20,000," one office employee commented, "but all of a sudden, I can buy office supplies, pay someone for translations, go to that conference."[12] It also enjoyed better communication with the mayor's office, as staff members were invited to participate in Mayor Parker's monthly senior staff meetings. These changes effectively recast MOIRA staff as well-protected civil servants, one office employee commented, rather than "mayoral appointees who could be fired any time."[13]

Soon after the reorganization, MOIRA staff and its MACIRA partners set out to rename and rebrand the office to stave off critics on the city council and in the public and to strengthen ties with the city's powerful business community. Because even including the word "immigrants" in MOIRA's name was a red flag, they renamed MOIRA the Office of International Communities (OIC) in 2011, a nod to the oil and gas companies that have given Houston a "world presence."[14] "We needed to change our image, we needed to rebrand ourselves," one office employee said, "so we can change people's negative attitudes about immigrants in this pretty conservative city."[15] Mayoral staff opted for OIC because it signaled that Houston was open to international business and because, as one office employee explained, "anything 'international' is the caviar of government; it's more exotic."[16] Another office employee added that "we didn't have too much interaction with [the business community] in the first years of opening [MOIRA]," which he saw as a missed opportunity to build acceptance and support for the office.[17] MACIRA was similarly renamed the Advisory Council of International Communities (ACIC) and granted 10 additional seats for members from the business community, which had disengaged from the advisory council during the final years of the White administration.[18]

The office renaming was a direct appeal to business-friendly conservatives who were uneasy with the office's previous focus on helping immigrant day laborers, as well as players in the international market who stood to benefit from its new focus on welcoming trade with international communities within and outside Houston. And while many community partners welcomed the office's renaming and ACIC's expanded membership, some did not. A staff member of Boat People SOS, the southwest Houston branch of a national immigrant organization originally founded to serve Vietnamese refugees, voiced one typical concern. The rebranding was "a political move, a financial move," he commented.[19] "They brought in the businesses to get more support," he added, "but it felt like we were continuing to marginalize even further the communities that we, the nonprofits, were representing."[20]

These objections notwithstanding, in 2011 and 2012, OIC and ACIC engaged in a strategic planning process to ensure that the office would meet the needs of Houston's diverse immigrant communities through programs and initiatives palatable to conservative city council members and local business leaders. This process identified new priority areas for OIC, such as language access. OIC and ACIC convinced Mayor Parker to sign an executive order in 2013 requiring city departments to offer services in the five most commonly used foreign languages in Houston to help break down language barriers in city government, a move befitting "an international city of commerce, culture, trade, travel, and tourism" (City of Houston 2013a). OIC also focused on fighting human trafficking, a central concern for local advocates and a funding priority of the federal Department of Justice (DOJ). Identified by the DOJ as one of the nation's largest hubs for sex and labor trafficking (HTRA 2022), Houston needed to support trafficking victims, according to OIC. These concerns led to the creation of a widely supported Human Trafficking Unit in the Houston Police Department and a fund to help trafficking victims, creatively paid for with city fees imposed on the city's many notorious strip clubs.[21]

Following the Parker administration, Mayor Sylvester Turner, a Democrat and Houston's second Black mayor, narrowly won office in 2015. Entering with much goodwill toward OIC, Turner kept the office in the Department of Neighborhoods and maintained Benito Juárez and Terence O'Neill at the helm. Throughout his administration, Turner helped the office build external partnerships and validation. For example, with his support, OIC secured a technical assistance grant from Welcoming America, a Georgia-based nonprofit that helps cities nationwide become immigrant-inclusive communities. This collaboration prompted yet another name change, with OIC becoming the Office of New Americans and Immigrant Communities. ACIC was also renamed the Mayor's Advisory Council of New Americans. Furthermore, in 2016, Turner proclaimed Houston to be a "Welcoming City" and, with philanthropic support, formed a 39-member multisector task force to recommend city policies that promote immigrant integration (Welcoming Houston 2017). The 50 recommended interventions would promote immigrants' integration into the civic, social, and economic fabric of Houston. However, most require new legislation and (elusive) city council approval, and hence have yet to be implemented.

Overall, MOIRA owes its 2001 creation to a Democratic mayor who, responding to community pressures and needs, deployed a mayoral initiative without support from most city council members. The subsequent institutionalization of Houston's immigrant affairs office, however, has been a slow and bumpy process. This has been largely due to contentious relations between Democratic mayors and Republican city council members and their constituents, who consistently objected to a city office that, they argued, used public funding to cater to undocumented immigrants. The office's two-decade-long survival has in large part stemmed from eschewing support for these undocumented immigrants. Meanwhile, local immigrant activists have exerted consistent pressure on the mayor and Democratic city council members, as well as made compromises with the city's conservative and business-friendly base, to keep the office around.

"One of the biggest accomplishments," one office employee commented in 2012, "is that we are still here and the programs are still going," adding that "before the office was open, it was hard for any mayor to get any idea what immigrants and refugees were out there or even understand their issues."[22] Democratic mayors have leveraged the city's strong executive system to protect the office against its many critics, and immigrant and other community organizations have worked with the office to develop programs with broad appeal that sidestep contentious issues related to undocumented immigrants. Notably, these include launching monthly Citizenship and Immigration Forums, promulgating a citywide language access policy, and establishing a Human Trafficking Unit. With only two full-time staff, a small programmatic budget, and a narrow, politically fraught mission, these are impressive accomplishments. They nonetheless pale in comparison to the initiatives that the immigrant affairs offices of other big cities have advanced (de Graauw 2018). What, we should ask, could the leadership of Houston's immigrant affairs office have done with a more supportive city council and more plentiful resources?

Though the Houston city council remains divided on immigrant issues, several recently elected council members have acknowledged that Houston's growing diversity necessitates some form of immigrant affairs office. Council member Mike Laster (2012–2018), who proudly referred to his District J in southwest Houston as the "Ellis Island of the city," explained that an immigrant affairs office gives the city's many immigrants "an immediate sense of respect."[23] Similarly, Ed Gonzalez, representing the immigrant-dense District H in northern Houston between 2009 and 2016 (before being elected sheriff of Harris County), lauded the office as "important because Houston was recently named the most diverse city in America."[24]

Curiously, though, neither Laster nor Gonzalez substantially engaged with the office or even knew much about its workings when they were in office.[25] This reflects the traditional laissez-faire and hands-off approach of Houston city politics. And while few council members today publicly oppose Houston's immigrant affairs office, many officials on both sides of the political aisle still embrace a small government ethos and contend that city government should not get involved in managing or promoting immigrant integration. Al Hoang, a Vietnamese immigrant who represented the immigrant-dense District F in western Houston between 2009 and 2014, believes that immigrant integration issues are best "handled by civic clubs and civic organizations."[26] Many other council members, Democrats and Republicans alike, similarly stressed that the needs of Houston's immigrants should be addressed by private sector organizations, without a commitment of much city funding.

Houston's and Harris County's Involvement in Federal Immigration Enforcement

The evolution of Houston's immigrant affairs office highlights how *local* partisan opposition can limit how city officials address immigrant integration. Houston's immigration enforcement efforts instead reflect the influence of *state* and *federal* politics on local debates around immigrant exclusion and criminalization. In the United States, the federal government determines immigration policies, but state and local governments make up a "multijurisdictional patchwork" where these policies are implemented and contested

(Varsanyi et al. 2012). Nationwide, advocates' calls to legalize undocumented immigrants have been largely futile, and state leadership in Texas has demanded increased immigration enforcement at the state's international border and in its interior. In Houston, the vast underrepresentation of Latino residents and the high number of noncitizens ineligible to vote have made it challenging to push back against this federal and state enforcement regime. This national and state policy landscape, focused largely on immigrant detention and deportation, has also had a contradictory impact on Houston's approach to immigration enforcement.

Houston is a site of political contradictions and contestation on the immigration enforcement front. Given its proximity to the southern border and its status as a major hub for the migration industry (Hernández-León 2008), the Houston area is home to one of the largest undocumented populations in the country, estimated at 506,000 (Capps and Soto 2018).[27] In response to increased federal and state enforcement efforts, many Houston and Harris County officials have called for added resources with which to surveil, detain, and deport immigrants. Simultaneously, these efforts have caused a growing number of immigrant and labor organizations to counter these trends and contest local cooperation with federal immigration officials.

Three policies or movements highlight these dynamics: (1) a 1992 order to the Houston Police Department (HPD) that prohibits apprehending people solely on the suspicion that they might be illegally present in the United States, (2) a failed 1997 city council proposal to make Houston a "safety zone," and (3) multiple campaigns to fortify cooperation between local law enforcement and federal immigration officials through the federal 287(g) and Secure Communities programs. Together, these local immigration policy debates highlight the relevance of the region's mixed partisan context and the complexity of overlapping city-county jurisdictions with sometimes different approaches to immigration enforcement.

Immigration Enforcement in the City of Houston

For decades, Houston's string of Democratic mayors issued or supported directives that city police officers stay out of federal immigration enforcement. In 1992, several years before the 287(g) program became a legal reality, then Houston police chief Sam Nuchia—a Republican serving under Democratic mayor Bob Lanier—introduced General Order 500-5. This order stated that "[Houston police] officers shall not make inquiries as to the citizenship status of any person, nor will officers detain or arrest persons solely on the belief that they are in this country illegally" (HPD 1992). According to local immigrant rights supporters, this order was a matter of "public safety" and designed to build trust with immigrant communities. Immigration opponents, however, charged that it brought Houston closer to becoming a "sanctuary city" and a magnet for undocumented immigrants (Freemantle 2005).

In the wake of increased federal efforts to criminalize undocumented immigration in the mid-1990s, local advocates worked to strengthen immigrant protections in Houston. In 1997, immigration lawyer (and later city council member) Gordon Quan attempted, but failed, to institutionalize General Order 500-5 by making Houston a "safety zone," where undocumented immigrants could apply for city services and not be reported to federal immigration authorities. While police leadership argued that maintaining a buffer between federal immigration officials and city police officers was critical to building trust with immigrant communities, several rank-and-file officers contested the order. One Houston police officer even testified at a 2003 hearing of the immigration subcommittee of the U.S. House Committee on the Judiciary, arguing that his police work was hindered by not being able to query immigrants about their status (Murthy 2010). He and other opposing officers pointed to rare but high-profile crimes committed by undocumented residents to bolster their claims.

In 2005, Republican city council member Mark Ellis (in office from 2000 to 2006) attempted to force a vote to rescind the 1992 police order and instead pass legislation that would require Houston police officers to enforce federal immigration laws. With a background in finance and law enforcement, Ellis represented District F, which encompasses both the affluent residential and commercial west-side area of Houston and the working-class and immigrant southwest side. Ellis objected to Houston becoming a sanctuary city and charged, with no evidence, that Houston residents were being subjected to the crimes of undocumented immigrants drawn to the city because of the protective order (Freemantle 2005). While other Republican council members were equally critical of undocumented immigration, they were nonetheless divided about the role Houston officials should play in federal immigration enforcement. For example, M.J. Khan—a Pakistani American Republican who replaced Ellis as District F representative—publicly opposed undocumented immigration. Yet he also argued that it was the responsibility of "specially trained federal officials to check for valid visas and passports," citing racial profiling concerns if this was left to city police officers (Hegstrom 2005). Lacking a united Republican front and confronted with a strong community campaign in favor of the 1992 order, Ellis ultimately failed in his bid to rescind it.

Despite continued support for the 1992 HPD order through the 2000s, Houston at times came remarkably close to embracing the federal 287(g) enforcement program. Named after Section 287(g) of the federal Illegal Immigration Reform and Responsibility Act of 1996, this program encourages local (and state) law enforcement officials to collaborate with federal immigration officials, effectively turning them into immigration enforcement "force multipliers." While 287(g) agreements have been authorized since 1996, they attracted much more attention across the United States after the 2001 terrorist attacks (Rodríguez et al. 2010), including among Houston's political elite.

Harold Hurtt, Houston's police chief between 2004 and 2009, was initially a vocal critic of the 287(g) program. Hurtt argued that it would detract from the HPD's central mission and cut into scarce city resources. However, both he and Mayor Bill White, who had long supported the 1992 police order, felt increasing pressure to have the HPD collaborate with U.S. Immigration and Customs Enforcement (ICE) to identify and arrest Houston's undocumented immigrants. Militant anti-immigrant groups and council members like Michael Berry, who held an at-large council seat between 2004 and 2008 while also hosting conservative radio talk shows, called for the city to take a harder stance. In the spring of 2009, when an undocumented immigrant with a criminal record shot and critically injured a Houston police officer during a drug raid (Olson and Carroll 2009a), White's position shifted decisively toward enforcement first. White—who at the time aspired to run for statewide office—subsequently began to champion the 287(g) program.

Meanwhile, Police Chief Hurtt, who had been appointed by Mayor White, was seemingly conflicted over the program. He eventually gave his cautious support but would only allow HPD officers to check for immigration status in the city's two jails, not at random while on patrol. Explaining his decision, Hurtt cited the bureaucratic complexity the program would introduce and the thin line between fighting crime and effective community policing. "I don't want my guys out on the street trying to determine which of 32 different visas [is valid]," he said, adding, "I want them to concentrate on keeping Houston safe from thieves, drug dealers, sex offenders, and making sure we maintain the trust and support of everybody who lives in Houston, and that means members of the immigrant community we serve" (Pinkerton 2009a). Reservations aside, Hurtt and White both ultimately gave in to the strong conservative, pro-enforcement forces on the city council and among state and federal politicians. City officials who aspired to state or national office, like White and Hurtt, could not afford to be painted as too progressive on immigration. White would eventually lose the governor's race to Republican incumbent and immigration hardliner Rick Perry. Hurtt, ironically, next took a job as the assistant director of state and local coordination at ICE.

White and Hurtt faced harsh criticism, both from immigrant rights advocates who called their about-face on the 287(g) program "hypocritical" and from the police union and anti-immigration advocates who wanted HPD to have even more authority to ask about immigration status (Pinkerton 2009a). White held firm for the moment, but then changes in federal policy shifted the conversation in Houston. As proponents continued to push the 287(g) program as an important tool for maintaining law and order, it came under growing scrutiny nationally for the resulting widespread racial profiling. In March 2008, the Obama administration piloted a new enforcement tool called Secure Communities (S-Comm), a fingerprint program that allows ICE to check the immigration status of every person arrested and/or booked into the police station or state or local jail. The S-Comm program, which would become mandatory for all U.S. law enforcement jurisdictions in 2011, allowed Houston's political leadership to embrace enforcement measures that were more palatable to a conservative base. And since S-Comm was advanced by the Obama administration, it also gave them bipartisan cover and a way out of their 287(g) conundrum. Mayor White officially backed away from the 287(g) program in October of 2009 after negotiations with ICE broke down over program administration and cost (Carroll 2009). HPD began using the S-Comm fingerprinting databases in December 2009 (Selby 2010).

Mayor Annise Parker, White's Democratic successor, also shifted her stance on the 287(g) program. During her 2009 mayoral campaign, Parker had vowed to use the program in city jails, but she quickly backtracked once in office, citing cost concerns in a tight budget year (Carroll and Olson 2010). Parker opposed HPD officers checking for immigration status on the street but was also adamant that "Houston is not a sanctuary city; if you break a law in Houston, we will arrest you, we will take you to jail, and, if you're in this country illegally, we will turn you over to the appropriate federal agency, generally ICE" (Stiles 2010). It is unclear what impact this political maneuvering had on the lived experiences of Houston's immigrants, though advocates felt it fueled a climate of fear for immigrant communities. As city officials debated, embraced, and eventually abandoned a 287(g) agreement within the city, the program remained in force in Harris County for almost a decade, affecting many undocumented Houstonians who resided in Harris County.

Immigration Enforcement in Harris County

The larger Houston metropolitan region spans 13 counties, the largest of which is Harris County. Harris County encompasses most of the city of Houston and is denser and more politically progressive than its surrounding counties, yet it has also been the top U.S. county for ICE arrests over the past several years (TRAC 2018). According to the Houston Immigration Legal Services Collaborative, "ICE arrests in Harris County account for more than a quarter of all ICE arrests in Texas, even though the county constitutes only 16 percent of the state's population" (HILSC 2020b). As such, any examination of immigration enforcement in Houston must also contend with the specific political dynamics of Harris County, which is a site of pronounced contestation around immigrant issues *and* has a long legacy of promoting immigration enforcement efforts.

In July 2008, as Houston city officials were rethinking their adherence to the federal enforcement program, Harris County signed a 287(g) agreement to allow its sheriff's deputies to collaborate with ICE officials. The Harris County Sheriff's Office is the main police force for the unincorporated areas of its jurisdiction but can still exercise authority in all areas of the county under Texas law, including in the city of Houston (HCSO 2023; TAC 2023). While recent Houston city police chiefs were all appointed by Democratic mayors, Harris County sheriffs are independently elected and thus enjoy freedom to support enforcement policies like 287(g). In fact, support for the 287(g) program became a cornerstone for sheriffs' election and reelection campaigns in Harris County, whose electorate, while more progressive than nearby counties, is still more conservative than that of the city of Houston. In Harris County, support for the 287(g) program also served as a marker of commitment to law and order among its five legislative county commissioners.

Following the terrorist attacks of September 11, 2001, Harris County Sheriff's Office personnel merely asked inmates to voluntarily disclose their immigration and citizenship status. Toward the end of his term in 2008, however, Republican sheriff Tommy Thomas (in office 1995–2008) directed his personnel to undergo federal training to proactively identify undocumented inmates, becoming the first Texas jurisdiction to do so. Thomas later sought permission from the Harris County Commissioners Court to enter into a 287(g) agreement, arguing that ICE lacked adequate resources to enforce immigration laws on its own and that the program would help reduce crime in the county. "In a perfect world, I'd like to see our borders secured to where [if] we have someone we find to be here illegally, we turn them over to ICE and have them deported," he explained, adding, "but that's not something that's happening at this day and time" (Carroll and Davis 2008).

Immigration enforcement became a centerpiece of Thomas's reelection bid, but he eventually lost his seat to Adrian Garcia, a Democrat who had represented the immigrant-dense District H in northern Houston since 2004. Harris County's 287(g) policy persisted for some time, even under Garcia, who was the county's first Hispanic sheriff and was once described as a "son of legal immigrants" who had moderated on immigration issues while on the Houston city council (Grissom 2010). Garcia initially promised to reevaluate the county's participation in the 287(g) program. However, instead he requested its renewal in 2009, despite vocal opposition from community advocates who criticized the program's civil rights and racial profiling abuses.

Sylvia Garcia, the sole Hispanic Democratic county commissioner, was the only one to vote against the extension, with the other four White Republican commissioners supporting it.

The danger of the 287(g) program, advocates warned, was the one-two punch of racial profiling that made it all but certain that you would be pulled over when "driving while brown." One leader of a Mexican advocacy organization explained that "sometimes the sheriff's officers stop people because of color; they stop you because they look brown," adding that "even if they got a sticker, the car plate, they stop them and they take them to their jail."[28] Sheriffs like Garcia have long defended the program by noting that it catches immigrants who have committed serious crimes. Yet many investigative reports have confirmed that it is not just felons who get fast-tracked to deportation proceedings. Even benign traffic stops can put immigrants on this path quickly and with little recourse (Armenta 2017). One news report on the Harris County 287(g) program noted that "less than 10 percent of those caught in the ICE screening fit the profile of serious criminals" (*Houston Chronicle* 2009). Because of the 287(g) program, Harris County became a major cog in the federal deportation machine, earning Houston the label of "deportation capital" of the United States (Duong 2016).

In light of significant criticism, in 2010, Sheriff Garcia appointed a 13-member citizen committee to advise him on the treatment of undocumented immigrants in county jails. This was a nominally progressive move, but community advocates criticized the committee's lack of diversity and the notable underrepresentation of grassroots community interests. "Is this committee going to protect the interests of the office of the sheriff," one local advocate asked, "or is it going to represent the interests of the immigrant community?" (Moran 2010). They perhaps had reason to be skeptical, as in 2013 Garcia once again backed renewing the 287(g) program, which this time was unanimously approved by the commissioners court. As a result, nine Harris County law enforcement officials would continue to work alongside ICE agents in identifying, arresting, and deporting undocumented immigrants from county jails. When Garcia was asked in 2012 during his reelection campaign whether he would continue to support the 287(g) program, he bluntly and strategically responded, "I continue to support it; it is an important security program," adding that "the only way in which I will always apply it is in the jail. We will not go out looking for people with questionable immigration status to arrest them for that alone" (Struthers 2012).

When Garcia stepped down as sheriff in 2015 to run (unsuccessfully) for mayor of Houston, Republican Ron Hickman replaced him on an interim basis. His enforcement policies were notably harsher than Garcia's, "annihilating all the modest progress of his predecessor," as one community activist described the transition.[29] The same activist characterized Hickman as completely nonresponsive to community organizations, making time only to comment to major media outlets. She also characterized him as inconsistent and seemingly confused on the implications of his policies. She stated, "At the very beginning of our campaign [to end the 287(g) program in Harris County], he told the *Houston Chronicle* that 287(g) did not exist anymore in Houston and that Harris County was not part of the 287(g) program. Most recently, from our last action, he said that 'we understand the public outcry of the 287(g) program, but we're doing as much as we can to work with it.' We don't think that he even understands."[30]

After only a year, however, Harris County voters returned a Democrat to the sheriff's office, this time former Houston city council member Ed Gonzalez, who as of this writing continues in the office. Gonzalez had campaigned on doing away with the controversial 287(g) program, a pledge he fulfilled in February 2017. Arguing that his decision was a resource allocation issue and not a political statement, Gonzalez said he would put the $675,000 that the county spent on the program annually toward addressing major crimes and other priorities.

Gonzalez's decision to end the county's participation in the 287(g) program came as newly elected president Donald Trump called for stronger interior enforcement and the expansion of local immigration enforcement programs. This charged federal context helps explain why Harris County finally ended the program. Just as the county started to turn bluer politically, Trump's new immigration policies catapulted local and statewide immigrant rights groups into action, with Houston area activists doubling down on advocacy to finally end Harris County's 287(g) program. The Houston Beyond ICE Coalition worked hard to build a broad base of supporters that included diverse communities of Houstonians disproportionately targeted by local law enforcement. The coalition involved not only immigrant rights organizations such as United We Dream and FIEL but also activists from Black Lives Matter Houston and SEIU's Fight for 15 and Justice for Janitors campaigns (Pandit 2016). These activists consistently spoke out against the 287(g) program during county commissioner hearings and creatively exerted pressure on county officials, staging a "die-in" in front of the Harris County Sheriff's Office and a Valentine's Day rally asking Sheriff Hickman to prove his love to Houston's immigrant community by ending the program.[31]

They finally prevailed in 2017, when county officials voted to end the 287(g) program. Since then, the partisan tides in Harris County have shifted, giving Democrats control of the five-member commissioners court. It is not yet clear, however, what this shift means for immigrant rights. Republican judge Ed Emmett, who headed the county commissioners between 2007 and 2019, strongly defended the 287(g) program as a commonsense tool for law and order. "Do I think 287(g) is the best way?" he asked. "I have no idea. I'm not in law enforcement, but do I think that if somebody gets arrested for a real crime . . . then should our law enforcement people check with all databases to see if they're wanted for anything else? Absolutely."[32] Today, Emmett's seat is filled by Democrat Lina Hidalgo, a political newcomer born in Colombia who—as part of the Democratic wave elected in 2018—narrowly defeated incumbent Emmett when she was only 27 years old (Zaveri 2018). Hidalgo has helped funnel over $2 million to a countywide immigrant defense fund to aid immigrants facing deportation (Hansen 2020). Yet, despite Hidalgo coming to power, progress on immigrant rights remains halting. In recent years, for example, Harris County (as well as Houston) officials have lauded the opening of a joint inmate processing center where ICE, among other law enforcement agencies, continues to enjoy office space and access to records.

In short, immigration enforcement in Houston faces a complex policy landscape: overlapping jurisdictions, ever-shifting federal directives, conflicting city and county policies, slowly changing local electorates, and, more recently, state bills targeting undocumented immigrants across the state. In this environment, the HPD has taken a more inclusive approach, largely because its chief—unlike the Harris County sheriff—is appointed and not directly beholden to voters. However, the persistent association between immigration policy and supposed immigrant criminality across all levels of government and public debate across the United States has required Houston officials to navigate between advocacy from immigrant rights supporters and opposition from conservative nativists.

Public-Private Collaborations to Implement Federal Immigration Benefits

While often addressing enforcement, federal policies also provide some important immigration benefits, including temporary protection from deportation, work authorization, permanent residency, and U.S. citizenship. Successfully implementing these benefits requires targeted outreach to immigrant communities and the financial, staff, and technical resources to process immigrant applications. In the absence of federal funding for these activities or coordination of these benefits to immigrants, local governments and civil society actors around the country have long assumed key implementation roles (e.g., Bloemraad 2006; Hagan and Baker 1993).

Given its large number of foreign-born residents, finding the resources to implement federal immigration benefits is particularly critical in Houston. These residents include 244,000 immigrants eligible for naturalization, a process that requires them to demonstrate English-language proficiency and a basic knowledge of U.S. history and government (CSII 2016). Applicants must also pay a hefty filing fee, which as of 2024 is $710 if they file for naturalization online and $760 if they use a paper application. An estimated 196,000 undocumented immigrants in Houston are also eligible for temporary relief from deportation under President Obama's 2012 DACA and 2014 Deferred Action for Parents of Americans and Lawful Permanent Residents (DAPA) programs (CPPP 2016). These programs were narrowly defined, confusing to many, and announced with little time for immigrants to adequately prepare. It thus fell on local community organizations to provide crucial information to immigrants and help them apply. In contrast to their relatively more progressive colleagues in San Francisco, Chicago, and New York City (de Graauw, Gleeson, and Bada 2020), Houston officials have committed little public funding to implement immigration benefits programs and are particularly reticent in supporting undocumented immigrants. They have, however, elevated the efforts of local nonprofit organizations and philanthropy in this space.

Collaborations to Promote U.S. Citizenship

Houston city officials have consistently promoted the U.S. citizenship program for almost two decades. Because this program concerns legal immigrants, the city's stance and involvement have not been controversial. However, given the lack of public funding dedicated to immigrant integration—and social services more broadly—city officials have had to rely heavily on local nonprofits. In 2006, MOIRA teamed up with Neighborhood Centers, Inc. (NCI) to organize several Immigration Forums.

Founded in 1907, NCI, now called BakerRipley, is one of the oldest and largest nonprofits in Houston. Like the famous settlement houses of the northeast, BakerRipley has long provided educational and social programs for immigrants. Today, it draws on mostly federal and state government grants as well as more modest United Way funding, program fees, and donor contributions to offer an array of social services to low-income residents through its network of over 60 service sites throughout the Houston region (BakerRipley 2022). As part of the Immigration Forums, NCI supplied resources to promote citizenship, spaces to hold citizenship events, and volunteers, while MOIRA, as one NCI employee commented, provided "public legitimacy" and a means of "shar[ing] the news of what we were doing with city council and other city officials."[33] The early forums in this collaboration were mostly information sessions, educating immigrants about the citizenship process and providing referrals to legal services providers that could help them complete their applications.

In 2007, when U.S. Citizenship and Immigration Services (USCIS) nearly doubled the naturalization fee from $330 to $595, the National Association of Latino Elected Officials (NALEO) joined the city of Houston's partnership with NCI. NALEO had opened its Houston office in 1993, and from the beginning, it had offered four or five group-based workshops annually to help immigrants prepare and submit their citizenship applications. The now-expanded partnership with three key actors, renamed Citizenship and Immigration Forums, not only educated immigrants about U.S. citizenship but also guided them through the application process with the help of vetted attorneys. Barack Obama's 2008 presidential election fueled a national push to naturalize immigrants and "awaken the sleeping giant" that was the Latino vote (Ayón 2009). One NALEO employee similarly explained that they joined the MOIRA-NCI collaboration in Houston "to put our workshops on steroids to get ready for the 2008 presidential elections," adding that "we wanted all these people to become naturalized so they could participate in the elections, and we were going to make history."[34] The same NALEO employee referred to this collaboration as a "dynamic and effective partnership" with impressive outcomes.[35]

In 2010, two years after MOIRA, NCI, and NALEO formalized their partnership with a memorandum of understanding, the program conducted 15 large-scale forums that drew over 4,800 immigrants and resulted in the submission of almost 1,400 citizenship applications. Immigration attorneys contributed 300 pro bono hours, and other volunteers donated over 4,500 hours to the forums (MOIRA 2011). Since then, more supporting organizations have contributed time, staffing, information and outreach, and financial support to the now monthly forums, increasing the number of immigrants served. New partners include Univision (the largest provider of Spanish-language media content in the United States), USCIS (the federal agency charged with processing citizenship applications), the South Texas College of Law, and several immigrant organizations.[36]

In 2011, the city of Houston joined the New Americans Campaign (NAC), a national network of nonpartisan legal services providers, immigrant and faith-based organizations, foundations, and community leaders, to further expand naturalization assistance in the Houston metropolitan region. NAC membership provided the existing public-private citizenship alliance access to technical assistance funded by national foundations (such as the Carnegie Corporation and the Open Society Foundations) and local funders (notably the Houston Endowment) to grow local capacity to help legal immigrants navigate the citizenship process. This allowed the collaborative to better serve immigrants in Houston's underserved outlying areas. For example, one partner, Bonding Against Adversity (BAA), was created in 2010 to promote the economic development of the Aldine suburban area just north of Houston, home to many low-income immigrants.[37] With funding and technical support from NAC and NALEO, BAA has been able to offer regular citizenship workshops in their suburban service area (NAC 2014).

What started in 2006 as a MOIRA-NCI collaboration to inform immigrants about U.S. citizenship has grown into a well-oiled cross-sectoral partnership among the city government, nonprofit legal services providers, immigrant organizations, ethnic media, and local and national funders collaborating to offer free citizenship workshops year-round to immigrants in the greater Houston area. While the city government provides no public funding for these programs, its continued partnership has legitimized the workshops and increased their visibility among Houston's large population of naturalization-eligible immigrants.

There are certainly tensions in this alliance, according to one NALEO employee, as partners occasionally squabble about "how funding gets allocated, what are the best service models, and who reports to whom."[38] Their continued collaboration, however, does give immigrants access to quality and trusted legal services for naturalization throughout Houston. The popularity of this public-private partnership to promote citizenship is due in large part to its focus on legal immigrants, who are widely viewed as net contributors to Houston's economy.[39] "This is a city driven a lot by business interests, and we often frame things in what is good for the economy," one local advocate commented on the campaign's strategy.[40] Whereas naturalization campaigns in other cities have often focused on strengthening democracy and increasing immigrant civic engagement, framing the citizenship workshops in Houston in economic terms "has helped to get many people on board to make them happen."[41]

Collaborations to Promote DACA and DAPA

In contrast to their support of citizenship assistance, Houston city officials have played almost no role in promoting DACA or DAPA. DACA, a 2012 initiative of President Obama, provides a temporary (two-year) and renewable stay of deportation and work authorization to young *undocumented* immigrants who meet criteria related to age, educational achievement, continuous U.S. presence, and lack of criminal history. This population, while often viewed as the most deserving of some sort of immigration relief, has been a political firebrand. U.S. Attorney General Jeff Sessions immediately challenged and eventually rescinded the program in 2017, though it has benefitted over 835,000 young undocumented immigrants nationwide (DHS 2023b). Several state governors, including Texas's Greg Abbott, supported his challenge, and they would later lead their own. The U.S. Supreme Court overturned the DACA rescission in 2020, but ongoing appeals and litigation have meant that the

DACA program is available only for the initial beneficiaries. The broader DAPA program proposed in 2014 sought to provide relief to an additional 4.5 million undocumented parents of U.S. citizen and green-card-holding children but was never implemented. Nonetheless, the hopeful period before DAPA evaporated motivated immigrant advocates in Houston to help prepare immigrants for the possibility that relief might be on the horizon.

Local government and civil society organizations in immigrant gateways like San Francisco and New York City extended their naturalization partnerships and existing resource and referral systems for immigrant and refugee services into collaborations around promoting DACA and DAPA. This did not happen in Houston. Civil society leaders identified the stigma facing undocumented immigrants in Houston as a key reason why such cooperative campaigns failed to materialize. "A big issue, especially with DAPA," one foundation employee commented, "was the local politics of allowing adult individuals who knowingly entered this country illegally to get some kind of legal status."[42] She added, "It's really hard for the mayor to get support from city council members to fund the implementation of these programs, even among Democrats, who tend to be on the more conservative side in Texas."[43] Republicans also framed their staunch resistance to promoting DACA and DAPA as a defense of local rule. For example, some city council members equated the DACA and DAPA programs with presidential overreach, an argument central to the Texas-led lawsuits against both programs. "City council might have been supportive of [DACA and DAPA]," one local advocate commented, "if they had gone through the proper legislative procedure, had they not been created by executive action."[44]

Two local foundations—the Houston Endowment and the Simmons Foundation—stepped into the local leadership vacuum to coordinate local DACA and DAPA implementation efforts amid broader efforts to prepare for the possibility of a mass legalization program. In early 2013, a grantor-grantee dialogue on immigration organized by the United Way of Greater Houston alerted these foundations to the acute need for expanded immigration legal services in Houston, especially if comprehensive immigration reform should finally come to pass. "I still remember that the head of Catholic Charities stood up during that meeting," one foundation employee recounted, "and said that comprehensive immigration reform would have a tsunami effect in our community because right now, [even] without any formal legislation, legal services providers were able to meet the needs of only 20 percent of the people coming in for immigration services."[45]

Following several more informal conversations with local legal services providers, the Houston Endowment and the Simmons Foundation decided in February 2013 to invest a modest $150,000 to set up the Houston Immigration Legal Services Collaborative (HILSC). HILSC brings together local legal services providers and university law clinics working with immigrant communities in Houston—notably Catholic Charities, Tahirih Justice Center, Boat People SOS, YMCA International Services, BakerRipley, Kids in Need of Defense, Memorial Assistance Ministries, South Texas College of Law, and the University of Houston Law Center Immigration Clinic—to create a coordinated network to assist low-income immigrants in accessing quality information and legal services.

HILSC used this initial funding to hire two part-time staff and commissioned the Migration Policy Institute—a nonpartisan, DC-based think tank focused on immigration issues—to produce a report on Houston's diverse immigrant population and help delineate the scope of immigration legal services needed in the Houston area (Capps and Soto 2018). HILSC also used the grant to commission services from the Catholic Legal Immigration Network, Inc. (CLINIC), a national organization focused on expanding affordable and quality legal representation to immigrants, especially in rural and suburban areas. CLINIC trained 100 local nonattorney nonprofit employees for accreditation by the U.S. Board of Immigration Appeals (BIA), enabling them to represent immigrants before U.S. immigration authorities. It also assisted six local nonprofits in gaining official recognition from the BIA, a strategy long used by advocates to multiply the limited supply of legal advocacy resources by relying on paralegal experts working under a supervising attorney. At the time, there were only 23 BIA-accredited individuals in Houston, reflecting the Houston metropolitan area's insufficient legal capacity, which has been amply demonstrated by Kerwin and Millet (2022). The HILSC initiative thus led to a significant and rapid increase in available trained personnel, which was crucial because hiring expensive immigration lawyers was just an impractical solution to Houston's enormous legal services problem.[46] Expanding the number of BIA-accredited representatives, one HILSC coordinator explained, was also a "way to empower immigrant women of color, because it's a mechanism for a much wider variety of people to be able to practice immigration law without having to go to law school."[47]

Using an unprecedented fast-track funding process usually reserved for major disaster relief, the Houston Endowment allocated $1.2 million in 2014 to allow local nonprofits to expand legal services capacity, improve and streamline immigrant access to existing services, and improve communications between legal services providers and other immigration stakeholders in the Houston area. Together, these three pillars of action constituted the community plan that HILSC members had collaboratively created in 2014 (HILSC 2015). Through an innovative participatory grant-making process, legal services provider representatives on HILSC's Executive Committee vetted the applications from fellow providers and allocated funding accordingly. Ultimately, 14 local organizations received funding to conduct outreach to immigrants about DAPA and help eligible immigrants apply for DACA. The following year, the Houston Endowment and the Simmons Foundation successfully attracted about $380,000 in matching funds from the Ford and the Open Society Foundations to continue their capacity-building work.[48] In subsequent years—and throughout the COVID pandemic—HILSC has continued to attract local and national philanthropic support to expand holistic immigration legal services in the Houston area. This support has benefitted a range of immigrants in Houston, including undocumented immigrants in detention, asylum seekers, and immigrants impacted by natural disasters and public health crises (e.g., HILSC 2020a, 2021).

This collaboration, according to one foundation employee, has created a "deeper trust" between local funders and the 14 to 27 organizations whose work HILSC funds annually.[49] Thanks to HILSC, another foundation employee noted, there is now "more collaboration and less competition among different legal services providers" to identify and address service gaps and find solutions to systemic shortcomings in the provision of immigration legal services in Houston.[50] Service providers now have more capacity to help immigrants, and the quality of immigration legal services in Houston's outlying areas has improved as well. In 2015, for example, Catholic Charities was able to open a legal services clinic in Fort Bend County, a swing county, often leaning Republican and located southwest of the city of Houston, with a large immigrant population that previously had no immigration legal services providers. The Houston Endowment even successfully engaged the George Foundation, a conservative, place-based funder in Fort Bend County with little prior "technical expertise around immigration legal services issues," to support some aspects of this new clinic.[51]

Given the context, the creation of HILSC was a remarkable feat. While it is not surprising that the Simmons Foundation, a small private foundation created in 1993 to build power in marginalized communities, supported HILSC, it was an unprecedented move for the Houston Endowment. A large private foundation founded in 1937, the Houston Endowment is "a very old, very established, and very conservative grant-making institution that is governed by a politically conservative board," explained one HILSC coordinator.[52] The Houston Endowment, however, has had a politically progressive management team that has framed their work with HILSC in a way that is palatable to its conservative board. One Houston Endowment employee emphasized that funding for DACA and DAPA implementation was "not about politics, but about the real lives of folks whom we're impacting," adding that the CEO and VP of programs provided "information to the board around what temporary status does to the socioeconomic conditions of individuals impacted by DACA and their families."[53] Sensitive to alienating potential conservative donors—with their perennial aversion to promoting undocumented immigration—HILSC has focused on legal services provision rather than political advocacy on behalf of undocumented immigrants. Not only does political advocacy "strike fear in the heart of every foundation, especially in Texas," one foundation employee explained, but faith-based legal services providers in HILSC—notably Catholic Charities and Memorial Assistance Ministries—did not want to be advocacy organizations.[54] HILSC thus has to walk a fine line in soliciting foundation support.

In all, local philanthropy has played a key role in organizing and expanding immigration legal services in the greater Houston area in the wake of DACA and DAPA. The city government, by contrast, did little to implement these federal initiatives, merely developing and hosting a multilingual website with information about President Obama's immigration initiatives in early 2015, when confusion over the fate of the DAPA program was at its peak. At a February 2015 city hall press conference revealing the website, Mayor Annise Parker—flanked by members of HILSC and several city council members—delivered a narrowly tailored message about the importance of Houston's immigrants receiving "accurate, complete information from trusted sources" to avoid immigration scams and fraud at the hands of unscrupulous providers, such as *notarios*,[55] who might try to take advantage of immigrants while DAPA was enjoined in court. This city website was not operational for very long, and today, it has fallen to HILSC to provide comprehensive online information about trusted legal services providers to whom Houston's immigrants can turn for help.

Strange Bedfellows Promote Immigrant Worker Rights

Progressive cities with an abundance of civic organizations usually generate immigrant rights advocacy collaborations between ideologically synchronous organizations (e.g., de Graauw 2016). In Houston's politically mixed and civically thin context, however, such coalitions necessarily require organizations with quite different ideologies and goals to collaborate. Efforts to protect the workplace rights of immigrants, for example, have required Houston labor, immigrant rights, and faith organizers to find strategic support from business leaders, often the quintessential foe in labor organizing campaigns. And yet, unlikely though it may be, this collaboration of strange bedfellows enabled Houston to become the first Texas city to adopt a policy against wage theft. Immigrant worker advocacy has notably evolved, from the failed minimum wage campaign in 1997 to the unexpectedly successful Down with Wage Theft campaign in 2013. This evolution shows how civil society organizations that were ideologically at odds have managed to work together—often precariously—to eventually score an important win for Houston's immigrant workers.

The fight for immigrant workers' rights in Houston is also nested within federal and state labor policy contexts that are a confusing labyrinth of agencies and jurisdictions, especially for immigrant workers who may lack English fluency or experience in navigating U.S. bureaucracies. Even the specific arena of wage and hour protections necessitates a familiarity with numerous statutes and agencies. The federal Fair Labor Standards Act, originally enacted in 1938, sets basic minimum wage protections that the Wage and Hour Division of the U.S. Department of Labor enforces. This statute covers all wage workers, regardless of immigration status, and formal memoranda of understanding about worksite enforcement activities between the U.S. Department of Homeland Security and the U.S. Department of Labor are supposed to maintain a nominal firewall between immigration and labor enforcement authorities.[56] While some states, including California and New York, have created even stronger immigrant protections against employer retaliation, others, like Arizona, have further entrenched the role of immigration enforcement at the workplace. Texas sits somewhere in between, in part because labor agencies recognize that doing immigration enforcement work requires scarce resources and results in mission drift (Gleeson 2014).

Texas is a challenging state for labor rights, especially for immigrant workers. As a "right to work" state, which weakens labor power, it has one of the lowest rates of union membership in the country: 3.8 percent, compared to 10.3 percent of all U.S. workers (BLS 2022). Union membership in the Houston metropolitan area is even lower at 3.0 percent (Hirsch and Macpherson 2022), and business-friendly policies have long been a key part of the city's brand. Texas labor laws have strengthened federal standards somewhat: in 2011, Republican governor Rick Perry signed SB1024, the so-called Wage Theft Bill, to increase the penalties for nonpayment of wages. However, the Texas Workforce Commission (TWC) still has limited power to implement and enforce these protections (McPherson 2011). Additionally, TWC's scarce resources largely concentrate on the state capital of Austin, leaving an enforcement vacuum throughout the rest of Texas. Furthermore, state policy prohibits Texas cities and counties from setting their own wage rates, though they can improve the enforcement of existing labor policies and worker rights (CIWO and CLASP 2020).

Just as local immigrant rights and labor advocates elsewhere in the United States have sought solutions to the lack of workplace regulations (e.g., Luce 2004), Houston advocates have attempted to strengthen these modest state efforts. In Houston, however, the region's thin civil society infrastructure has weakened immigrant worker advocacy power, with the lack of local government funding for labor standards enforcement further exacerbating the situation (Gleeson 2012). As we have seen, Houston bills itself as a place where businesses can thrive, free of zoning, excessive taxation, and unions.

"I think [Houston has] a very probusiness administration," one union leader soberly reflected, adding, "which is okay, but they also need to be pro-workers."[57] Indeed, business efforts in Houston have long focused on thwarting worker organizing, making it difficult for labor campaigns to gain traction. These challenges have required labor activists to devise innovative strategies that also benefit immigrant workers. One tactic has been to create alliances with "high-road"—even if not union-friendly—business leaders who wield notable power in Houston politics. Labor activists can then laud these employer allies for treating their workers well while employers can reap benefits through increasing the quality of their products and services with a well-paid and motivated workforce.

The story of wage theft protections in Houston begins with Proposition A, the failed 1997 initiative campaign to institute a living wage in Houston. Proposition A would have increased the city's living wage to $6.50, up from the federal minimum of $4.75. Bob Lanier—Houston's Democratic mayor from 1992 to 1998 who was once dubbed a "mogul-turned-politician" (Groves 1993)—stood firmly against it, and the proposition failed dramatically. This was a decisive moment for labor organizers, many of whom represented immigrant workers. Employers massively outspent advocates and took control of the narrative to sway public opinion against Proposition A (Gleeson 2012). For example, the media campaign from the opposition group Save Jobs for Houston Committee charged that the policy would lead to "Cops and firefighters [being] yanked off the streets. Higher taxes. Thousands of jobs lost. The wholesale destruction of small businesses. Streets riddled with potholes. Swollen welfare rolls" (Pollin et al. 2008, 6). In all, the business community spent about $1.3 million to defeat Proposition A, with $100,000 alone coming from the National Restaurant Association, while the AFL-CIO was only able to spend $20,000 in support of the initiative (Dyer 1996; Luce 2004).

In response to this defeat, and in an effort to blunt business lobbying power, advocates shifted their focus from an overall minimum wage to the labor rights of municipal workers and workers on city-funded contracts. Democratic mayor Lee Brown (1998–2004), more worker friendly than Lanier, responded to calls for city-led investigations into widespread abuses on construction sites at the new, city-funded Rockets basketball stadium and expanded convention center. Brown also built goodwill with labor leaders by increasing prevailing wages for workers on city contracts. After these successes, labor advocates attempted to combat wage theft more broadly, especially on Houston's many immigrant-dense construction sites. Efforts to allocate city resources toward day labor centers that could help fight wage theft were controversial and short lived, however. Thus, the problem of wage theft outside of city-funded construction projects continued to be widespread, with few tools to combat it (Gleeson 2013).

It was clear to Houston advocates that wage theft was a pressing problem affecting low-wage workers citywide. With few federal and state resources to address it, a solution demanded city intervention, especially since undocumented workers could not readily turn to federal or state officials for help. The U.S. Department of Labor only has authority in cases where workers are employed by corporations grossing over $500,000 a year or are otherwise engaged in interstate commerce. This jurisdictional mandate excludes many small employers, including most who employ immigrant day laborers. And even if accessing labor rights through federal bureaucracies were possible, immigrants often fear employer retaliation, do not want to become entangled with immigration enforcement, and lack a basic understanding of the claims process (Gleeson 2016; Griffith 2012). The TWC does have broader jurisdiction over labor violations, but it has relied largely on an inefficient phone claim system, with few to no in-person field offices outside of Austin.

In efforts to bypass these ineffective federal and state labor enforcement agencies, some Houston labor advocates engaged the Harris County Small Claims Court, an agency set up to address a range of disputes beyond labor issues. In some ways, this lowered the bar to file a worker claim, as one could do so without retaining an attorney or paying expensive fees. At the end of the day, however, this was a suboptimal means of addressing worker claims. "[This] process was voluntary," one Houston city official commented.[58] While the Harris County Dispute Resolution Center provided resources to try to alleviate the small claims court's overburdened docket, unrepresented workers are often inadequately prepared, and small claims courts tend to be unfamiliar with labor law (Thomas 2020). And workers who managed to go through the small claims court still had no real recourses because a judge could not compel employers to comply even if they had struck a deal with duped workers.

Confronted with these assorted challenges, local advocates sought other ways to deal with wage theft that harmed immigrant workers. In 2001, led by the local office of the federal Equal Employment Opportunity Commission, the community-based Justice and Equality in the Workplace Partnership (JEWP) launched in Houston (EEOC 2002). Federal agencies, the Mexican consulate, the Harris County AFL-CIO labor federation, the Houston mayor's office, and various nonprofit organizations collaborated through JEWP to inform immigrant workers of their rights and help them process claims through a consulate-hosted hotline (Gleeson 2012). This plan was sound in theory, but the problem, one organizer explained, was that the average immigrant worker knew nothing about how to reach JEWP providers.[59] Over time the JEWP hotline grew stagnant, and as one advocate explained, "we could never get that hotline staffed correctly at the Mexican consulate."[60] As both federal and state resources for JEWP waned over time, it became clear once again that there was a need for a more accessible labor rights enforcement bureaucracy at the city level, especially one that could effectively address the issues of wage theft in the city's booming construction industry.[61]

Police intervention has been possible for nearly two decades as another solution for addressing wage theft, but many advocates have been skeptical of its utility. In 2004, Houston police chief Harold Hurtt directed officers in his Burglary and Theft Division to respond to worker complaints of wage theft. This mechanism, however, required both a willing police officer to track down the offending employer and a district attorney willing to prosecute, not to mention a worker who knew how to get a police officer's attention. Even after significant outreach to and training for Houston police officers, many refused to devote time to wage theft, citing more serious crimes as priorities. "Think of it," one labor leader explained, "you're an average citizen, and you're trying to flag down an HPD officer, and you just had the window broken out in your car.... Who's he going to stop for?"[62] Additionally, immigrant workers were wary of approaching police officers. A community liaison officer in the HPD tried to build trust through regular visits to community organizations. However, many immigrants did not want to become entangled with police, and reports of police intimidating day laborers were common, making clear the necessity of a solution decoupled from law enforcement.[63]

In 2008, in the wake of yet another devastating hurricane (Hurricane Ike) that claimed the lives of 23 Houston-area residents, the Houston Interfaith Worker Justice Center (HIWJC) published a scathing report documenting wage theft abuses in Houston (HIWJC 2008). The report called on city officials and "high-road employers" to ensure that immigrant workers involved with post-hurricane debris removal, demolition, and reconstruction would not have their wages stolen. Mayor Bill White (2004–2010), a moderate Democrat with strong ties to the business community, offered little support during this campaign, focusing instead on humanitarian relief in the aftermath of the storm. Though he had won the endorsement of local unions, his move to balance the city's budget by cutting back on benefits for municipal workers placed the mayor's office once again at odds with labor leaders.

Labor activists, however, remained undeterred. In 2012, a HIWJC report doubled down on calls for city leadership to address the wage theft problem, profiling several notorious restaurants and construction businesses that routinely cheated immigrant workers out of their wages and calling on business allies to oppose wage theft to ensure fair competition (HIWJC 2012). Houston's Down with Wage Theft campaign soon received support from SEIU's Fight for a Fair Economy coalition, led by the newly formed *Fe y Justicia* Worker Center (formerly the HIWJC).[64] Advocates went door to door to gather signatures to get the wage theft issue before the city council, with Mayor Annise Parker ultimately agreeing to exercise her agenda-setting power to put forward a wage theft ordinance that would strengthen penalties for businesses committing wage theft and refusing to pay their judgments (Perez-Boston 2013). Supporters of the Down with Wage Theft campaign, dressed in iconic yellow T-shirts, repeatedly packed city council meetings to give testimony in support of the ordinance, which the city council unanimously supported in November 2013.

Beyond mayoral support, which is critical for enacting policies in a strong-mayor system like Houston's, the wage theft ordinance required buy-in from council members across the city's wide political spectrum. Mike Laster, a Democratic ally who represented the immigrant-heavy District J between 2012 and 2018, explained that getting the entire council on board with the ordinance required compromise on the part of labor and immigrant advocates. Advocates originally demanded that the city create an entirely new department dedicated to tackling wage theft. "We just simply did not have that capacity," Laster explained, "or the political backing to make that happen."[65] They compromised on a more limited policy focused on deterring employers from stealing workers' wages by banning offending employers from renewing their licenses to operate in the city of Houston (Morris 2013). This was framed as a commonsense approach to ensure fair business competition.

The influence and resources of the business community, especially several large construction firms, were key to this victory. Stan Marek, a well-known Houston construction magnate, had both material and moral motivations for supporting the wage theft ordinance. Marek, a faithful Catholic and proponent of "sensible immigration reform," was clearly frustrated with employers who steal wages from immigrant workers, thereby undercutting companies like his that do follow labor laws. "There are people making millions of dollars, big multibillion-dollar developers," he said, "they love cheap labor, my God."[66] The construction industry's bidding wars, he argued, relied on the seemingly limitless flow of undocumented workers, who became victims of developers' wage race to the bottom. This trend would push responsible business owners like him out and was a core driver (along with antiquated immigration policies) of wage theft in Houston. To succeed, though, Marek and politicians had to overcome certain fears, unfounded or not, of the business community. Then city council member Ed Gonzalez, representing the immigrant-dense District H in northern Houston between 2009 and 2016, discussed the anxieties he heard from business owners, who feared a "witch-hunt over just a frivolous [worker] complaint."[67] In turn, Marek and several of his sympathetic colleagues offered testimony at city council meetings and business gatherings, trying to allay the fears of other business owners opposed to greater government regulation.

Business leaders like Marek proved critical allies to the campaign, despite the inevitable tensions and disagreements they had with labor and immigrant rights leaders. The goal was always to "get responsible businesses on board," one labor advocate explained, but this necessitated setting aside differences over key labor organizing goals and visions for long-term immigration policy reforms.[68] "Sometimes you find yourself with strange bedfellows," the advocate dryly observed.[69] Coverage in the *Houston Chronicle*, the city's leading newspaper, succinctly summarized the Down with Wage Theft campaign's successful conclusion. "The seemingly easy [council] vote," it reported, "masked months of lobbying and negotiations among Mayor Annise Parker's administration, council members, workers' rights groups and business organizations" (Morris 2013).

While not mentioned in this *Houston Chronicle* quote, Houston faith leaders played an important mediating role in the Down with Wage Theft campaign. Indeed, much of the national movement to address wage theft emerged from interfaith networks that drew on the energy of local congregations and the moral influence of clergy (Bobo 2008). One Houston labor leader commented that faith leaders were an important part of a broader, multiactor advocacy strategy to fight labor abuses. "Just like any campaign where you have to come at the target from all different kinds of ways," he commented, "we [did] some media, but [also important was] having the faith community there, having pressure from the worker and their family, having the legal pressure from the small claims court." Notably, one worker center advocate commented, faith leaders could sway employers who were not "scared of the Department of Labor or the Texas Workforce Commission" to join the Down with Wage Theft campaign.[70]

Houston faith leaders also helped immigrant and labor advocates appeal to conservatives, arguing that protecting immigrant and worker rights was not a fringe progressive issue but one that squarely aligned with their religious convictions. Marek, for example, advocated both in Houston's construction industry and among the vast network of Catholic groups that provide immigration services throughout the city. This was not easy, explained one Catholic deacon who would frequently implore his parishioners that "virtually all immigration issues that we speak to are poverty issues as well."[71] Worker centers such as *Fe y Justicia* and the Metropolitan Organization also helped maintain strong ties between immigrant and labor leaders and Houston congregations. For years, unions and faith-based groups had conducted joint actions, riding together on the Justice Bus, which would roll through Houston calling out offending employers. This collaboration continued during the wage theft campaign, and the moral energy of the faith community both influenced council members during election season and helped secure the 2013 passage of the Wage Theft Ordinance (Thompson 2009).

As of March 2024, the City of Houston's Finance Department still formally enforces the Wage Theft Ordinance. An appointed wage theft coordinator has the power to process claims against businesses with city contracts and refer them to the TWC if necessary. The city, in turn, has built a wage theft database that tracks offending businesses, who can remove themselves from the list only when they have paid the assessed penalty. Noncompliant offenders can lose their city contracts and even their business license (City of Houston 2013b). Problems remain, however, with advocates complaining that the office is understaffed and ineffective. As of this writing, the department website lists a wage theft database with 453 entries of businesses in the larger Houston metropolitan area that have been convicted of and have an outstanding penalty for wage theft committed between April 2018 and August 2023 (City of Houston 2024). The coalition of labor, immigrant rights, and faith allies that came together to bring the ordinance to victory continues to rally for effective city oversight (UWU and EJC 2022).[72]

In sum, immigrant labor advocacy in Houston plays out within a complicated political context in which local politicians and business, labor, immigrant rights, and faith leaders have varying motivations. In this atmosphere, the compromise solution reached with Houston's Wage Theft Ordinance illustrates that framing is important when advancing immigrant rights issues. Rather than stressing wage theft as a core social justice issue for immigrant workers, the ordinance and the ensuing city government oversight aligned with the city's long-standing promise to advance fair business practices. A coalition of strange bedfellows came together to support the passage of the ordinance, drawing on the different nodes of social, economic, religious, and political power of Houston's immigrant rights and labor advocates, business leaders, and people of faith.

Conclusion

These four case studies demonstrate how Houston's challenging demographic, political, and civic contexts have slowed and shaped the contentious process of advancing immigrant rights in this southern gateway city. While affirming the importance of state-society relations and illustrating how weak political and civic interests can still exercise influence, these cases also show that no single formula works to ensure that governmental and nongovernmental actors can realize gains in immigrant rights.

Demographically, the hyperdiversity of Houston's foreign-born population defies a one-size-fits-all approach to advancing immigrant rights. Houston's immigrants have diverse national origins, immigration and citizenship statuses, language skills, socioeconomic profiles, and cultural backgrounds, making it complicated to define a coherent immigrant-friendly agenda. Immigrants are also spread widely across the metropolitan region, making it difficult for any centralized set of urban services to reach the immigrant-dense suburban neighborhoods ringing downtown Houston.

Politically, conservative forces in the city have been willing to accept policies and initiatives that advance the needs and interests of legal immigrants, such as naturalization support. Meanwhile, efforts to address key issues facing the city's many undocumented immigrants, such as the exploitation of day laborers, have been less popular. Republican city council members have traditionally embraced an enforcement-first approach to immigration policymaking, hampering local immigrant rights efforts. A small government ethos and lack of city funding have also prevented Houston from making major public programming investments, relying instead on philanthropy and civil society to fund, coordinate, and implement critical immigrant supports.

Finally, the overall infrastructure of immigrant-focused civil society organizations remains thin, and no one civil society organization has been able to advance immigrant rights on its own. Ideologically harmonious organizations, including immigrant-serving nonprofits, labor unions, and faith-based institutions, have had to collaborate consistently and over long periods of time to make any progress on immigrant rights. At times, they have also had to collaborate and compromise with business organizations, which are often on the opposite side of the ideological spectrum, to increase their chances of realizing inclusive policy change.

3

Cautious Optimism

The Future of Immigrant Rights in Houston

Advancing immigrant rights in Houston—a rapidly diversifying, politically mixed, and organizationally underserved gateway city—has been a slow and often contentious process. Progress has required a diverse set of governmental and nongovernmental actors to collaborate and strike difficult compromises. *What will the future of immigrant rights in Houston look like?* This chapter reflects on how recent changes in political leadership and policies at the federal and state levels have shaped local discussions and policy initiatives affecting Houston's immigrant communities. This chapter also speculates about the future of immigrant rights in a city whose population will soon become majority Hispanic and where the children of immigrants will join the city's civic and political life in greater numbers than their foreign-born parents did, the Democratic Party slowly is gaining ground in local elections, and the city's immigrant rights organizational infrastructure is maturing and expanding.

While there is reason for optimism, we caution that the future of immigrant rights in Houston will likely proceed along a rockier path than in other places that have experienced sustained international migration. The example of California, which has experienced high levels of immigration since the 1980s, is instructive. In 1994, during an economic recession and amid growing nativist sentiment, 59 percent of California voters approved Proposition 187, a controversial state initiative aimed at eliminating public benefits for undocumented immigrants. While Republican governor Pete Wilson, who endorsed Proposition 187, easily won reelection on a strong anti-immigrant platform, this Republican victory was short lived. Proposition 187 triggered a surge of new—overwhelmingly Democratic—Hispanic voters. At the same time, philanthropic organizations coordinated their resources to invest in, expand, and fortify a pro-immigrant infrastructure of community, labor, and social movement organizations that have constantly pressured state and local officials to advance immigrant rights (Colbern and Ramakrishnan 2020; de Graauw 2016). As a result, California turned from a purple to a solid blue state, and since the 2010s, the state's majority-Democratic policymakers have enacted a suite of pro-immigrant policies that have made it the most immigrant-friendly U.S. state today (Pham and Van 2021).

Houston will likely take a less decisive path forward, in part because the city's changing demography and state-level anti-immigrant policies like SB4 are unlikely to trigger a Democratic surge as they did in California. In today's post-Trump context, more Hispanics have shifted support *to*, not *from*, the Republican Party, a trend that is particularly visible in Texas and that gives Republicans hope that they will be able to blunt a rising Democratic advantage in the state's large cities (Sandoval and Goodman 2022). This trend may complicate the push for pro-immigrant policies in Houston, and furthermore, anti-immigrant federal and state policies will continue to constrain local government officials from enacting inclusive policies. Regardless, Houston's immigrant rights infrastructure is expanding, and local organizations will doubtlessly keep immigrant rights on the policy agenda. Because of ongoing community pressure, it seems likely that few local officials in Houston will publicly champion anti-immigrant measures or attack existing pro-immigrant ones. Yet progress on new local immigrant rights initiatives will likely continue to be contentious and slow.

Federal Politics and the Future of Immigrant Rights in Houston

The restrictionist, and often racist, tenor of federal immigration politics in the Trump era has seemingly faded but is being revived in the lead-up to the 2024 presidential election. Yet, early in his term, Democratic president Joe Biden issued new guidance on interior immigration enforcement that notably departed from the policies of the previous Republican administration. Instead of prioritizing all undocumented immigrants for removal, as President Trump did, Biden purportedly limited enforcement actions to immigrants who pose a national security risk, have been convicted of certain crimes, or recently entered the country illegally. He also formally limited the locations where interior enforcement actions can occur. Furthermore, Biden expanded Temporary Protected Status for immigrants, lifted Trump-era travel bans that applied largely to Muslim-majority countries, and rolled back "public charge" rules that have discouraged immigrants from using government benefits. Biden also attempted to end the controversial "Remain in Mexico" policy that kept asylum seekers from all over the world sequestered in Mexican border towns, living in desperate conditions while their asylum claims were slowly adjudicated in the United States (Chishti and Bolter 2022). As of this writing, however, ongoing court challenges have left the policy in place (Ables 2022; Mathur 2023). Finally, the controversial Title 42, a COVID-era policy from the Centers for Disease Control and Prevention that allowed for the swift expulsion of migrants at U.S. land borders to protect public health, finally expired in May 2023.

Overall, these have been welcome federal changes for Houston's immigrant rights advocates, many of whom had to spend scarce time and resources responding to various humanitarian border crises during the Trump administration. However, the federal focus on immigration enforcement has not fundamentally shifted. Border policies remain generally restrictive, with some analyses showing "no evidence that border enforcement has declined under Biden" (Fung 2022). Indeed, in May 2023, President Biden replaced Title 42 with a tougher and more restrictive "asylum ineligibility policy." This new policy bars nearly all asylum seekers who traveled through another country on their way to the southern U.S. border unless they (1) applied for asylum in one of those third transit countries and their application was denied or (2) managed to secure one of the limited appointments to enter at an official U.S. port of entry using a glitchy and flawed smartphone app known as CBP One (Robles 2023). In late July 2023, however, a federal judge struck this new asylum policy down for being "both substantively and procedurally invalid," a victory for advocates who sued the U.S. government, including the American Civil Liberties Union's Immigrants' Rights Project (Ainsley 2023; Jordan and Sullivan 2023). Meanwhile, however, interior enforcement efforts continue, with detention facilities—many located in and around Houston—remaining full and immigration courts severely backlogged (Arnold 2022).

Beyond enforcement issues, there continues to be congressional gridlock over potential reforms that would benefit the country's estimated 11 million undocumented immigrants. A permanent legislative solution to legalize and provide a path to citizenship for undocumented immigrants is particularly pressing given the ongoing battle over the DACA program in federal courts. As of this writing, the DACA program remains in legal limbo, permitting renewals but closing the program for first-time applicants who seek a temporary stay of deportation and work authorization. Additionally, because of age, entry restrictions, and program cutoff dates, DACA will soon cease being a tenable path for young undocumented immigrants currently graduating from high schools, considering college options, and looking to enter the workforce (Monyak 2023). In the Houston area—home to an estimated 506,000 undocumented immigrants (Capps and Soto 2018)—these realities are felt acutely, with the congressional stalemate over comprehensive immigration reform spurring local advocates to demand immigrant justice at all levels of government (Limehouse 2022).

Many Houston-area Republican members of Congress have taken strong anti-immigrant positions. While Senator John Cornyn—a Houston native in office since 2002—once actively supported a bipartisan bill to provide a limited legalization program, he has since abandoned this advocacy. Senator Ted Cruz, a Houston resident who has been in office since 2013, has built much of his career—including his 2016 presidential run—on a platform of expanding border and interior immigration enforcement. And Representative Dan Crenshaw, another loud national voice in office since 2019, is a proponent of border militarization and represents Texas's 2nd Congressional District, which includes Houston's affluent northern suburbs.

There have been some promising signs, though, for Democrats and their more inclusive immigrant agenda. While Republicans won a slim majority of House seats following the 2022 midterm elections, the Houston delegation continues to include several progressive voices who have championed comprehensive immigration reform. Among them are Democratic representatives Sheila Jackson Lee (18th Congressional District including central Houston), Al Green (9th Congressional District including southwest Houston), and Sylvia Garcia (29th Congressional District including eastern Houston). Immigration is sure to be a central issue in the reelection campaigns of all these Republican and Democratic federal officials who represent Houston, and their contrasting policy positions will continue to reverberate in Houston's local politics as well.

While federal officials continue to focus on immigration enforcement, the need for immigrant integration has begun to attract more notice (Bloemraad and de Graauw 2012). For example, USCIS has administered the Citizenship and Integration Grant Program since 2009, issuing modest federal grants to local organizations to provide citizenship instruction and application assistance to legal immigrants eligible for U.S. citizenship. Among the recipients are several Houston-based immigrant-serving organizations, including Boat People SOS, Catholic Charities, and BakerRipley, which have long worked with Houston city officials to offer monthly Citizenship and Immigration Forums (Trovall 2022b).

Additionally, long-running policies granting federal immigration prosecutorial discretion, which managed to fly under the radar during the Trump administration, have become further institutionalized under the Biden administration via two-year grants of deportation relief and work authorization. In January 2023, U.S. Department of Homeland Security (DHS) secretary Alejandro Mayorkas vowed to use these protections to hold "predatory actors accountable by encouraging all workers to assert their rights, report violations they have suffered or observed, and cooperate in labor standards investigations" (DHS 2023a). Advocates with the National Immigration Law Center and a coalition of labor organizations helped achieve these assurances and DHS policies that make workplaces safer and more equitable for immigrant workers (NILC 2021). Such federal policy shifts have helped advocates in Houston, many of whom seek to improve the conditions of low-wage workers in the city's construction and hospitality industries.

In the U.S. governmental system, where the federal government has exclusive power over immigration and citizenship issues yet different government levels increasingly have interrelated policy goals and administrative duties, the national enforcement-centered policy landscape will continue to shape how immigrant rights are discussed and legislated in Houston. Therefore, local officials in Houston can be expected to continue focusing on enforcement issues, with few incentives to address immigrant rights issues as well. This is true especially for local Republican officials who aspire to state or national elective office. As undocumented immigrants continue to find themselves in a federal legal limbo, local resources for addressing their needs and interests are more important than ever, notwithstanding the modest federal support there is for local organizations to promote naturalization among legal immigrants. This state of affairs will further galvanize local organizations to advocate for immigrant rights in Houston politics.

Texas Politics and the Future of Immigrant Rights in Houston

Beyond the contested federal terrain of immigration politics, Texas state politics remain firmly in conservative hands. This is reflected in a range of issues, including immigration. Republican governor Greg Abbott—a proponent of strengthening immigration enforcement and a lead architect of the court challenges against DACA—handily won (with 54.8 percent of the vote) his 2022 reelection against Democratic challenger Beto O'Rourke (44.8 percent). Nevertheless, O'Rourke outperformed Abbott in most urban counties, including Harris County, where O'Rourke (54 percent) beat Abbott (44.5 percent) by almost 10 percentage points (Politico 2023). Seeking to pressure the Biden administration to do more to restore order at the border, Abbott has been doubling down on his anti-immigrant positions, as evidenced by his recent Operation Lone Star that deployed the National Guard to deter unauthorized crossings on the Texas-Mexico border (Office of the Texas Governor 2022; Texas Military Department 2022). Abbott has also approved state contracts for border wall construction (García 2022) and, in mid-2023, signed into law a sweeping package of border security laws that as of this writing the nation's highest courts remain divided over (Office of the Texas Governor 2023). And along with Florida's Republican governor Ron DeSantis, he has sent asylum-seeking migrants on buses to northern sanctuary cities such as New York City and Philadelphia. In all, Texas's top executive official remains staunchly restrictionist, with a plurality of Texans approving of the job Abbott is doing (Texas Politics Project at the University of Texas at Austin 2023).

Conservative Republicans also continue to dominate the Texas state legislative leadership, and they have shown little support for a federal legalization program or a softened approach to asylum seekers. As of this writing, Republicans hold 19 of the 31 state senate seats and 86 of the 150 seats in the state house of representatives (Legislative Reference Library of Texas 2023). Texas's redistricting in 2021, controlled by Republicans, increased their hold on legislative offices and has been challenged under Section 2 of the federal Voting Rights Act in *Fair Maps Texas Action Committee v. Abbott* (2021) (Brennan Center 2022). The outcome of this case, alongside the 2026 statewide elections, will determine whether Texas will be redistricted more fairly in the wake of the 2030 Census.

Overall, conservative state policies have increasingly buttressed federal restrictions on immigrant arrivals while blunting federal efforts at immigrant inclusion. SB4, the 2017 Texas state law that effectively bans sanctuary cities, remains in effect. Republican Texas attorney general Ken Paxton has made good on his promise to sue localities that violate SB4, sending a clear warning to gateway cities like Houston that might otherwise push back against efforts at greater federal and state enforcement (Texas Attorney General 2022). This is part of a larger move by Republican state officials to try to restrict Democratic cities in Texas from passing a range of progressive policies, including local agriculture and labor laws that are more stringent than state (and federal) law (Scherer and Bureau 2023). Indeed, in mid-2023, they enacted (and Governor Abbott signed into law) the Texas Regulatory Consistency Act (HB2127), referred to by opponents as the "Death Star" law, which erodes the power of the state's bluer urban areas (Holder 2023). This state law likely means an end to Houston's Wage Theft Ordinance of 2013. Houston city officials have already sued the state in efforts to block this new law, arguing it violates the state's constitution (Fechter 2023).

Perhaps unexpectedly, several Texas policies that foster immigrant integration remain in place. Notably, the two-decade-old Texas Dream Act has enabled undocumented students to pay in-state tuition rates, making a college education more affordable for them. However, the anti-immigrant officials who have tried to dismantle the Texas Dream Act recently won a federal court case—*Young Conservatives of Texas v. University of North Texas* (2022). This case ruled that it was unconstitutional for Texas colleges to charge higher tuition fees for out-of-state citizens than for undocumented Texan students. This ruling could put pressure on Texas colleges to stop providing in-state tuition eligibility for Dreamers (IDRA 2022), which would create a significant integration barrier for the many undocumented youth in Houston. Meanwhile, a 2021 poll found widespread support for Dreamers among Texas registered voters: 87 percent of Democrats and even a 46 percent plurality of Republicans opposed the deportation of Dreamers (Ramsey 2021).

Partisan politics in Texas differ from other major immigrant-receiving states such as California and New York. Republicans are certainly more vocally anti-immigrant, but a bipartisan supermajority of the Texas Senate and House of Representatives favors restrictionist policymaking. According to the National Conference of State Legislatures, Texas enacted at least six bills with immigration implications in 2021. Only two were solely sponsored by Republican officials. Except for one law supporting U.S. veterans seeking to naturalize (SB886), the others strengthen immigration enforcement in one way or another. Collectively, these state laws increase resources for border security (HB9), increase penalties for smuggling undocumented immigrants (SB576), require "sexually oriented businesses" to use the federal employment verification program E-Verify (SB766), commission a study to create and maintain federal and state inspection facilities at all Texas ports of entry (SB1907), and regulate owners and operators of residential child detention facilities (SB2188) (NCSL 2022).

Texas's restrictive immigration and anti-Democratic city policies hem in Houston officials who might otherwise seek bolder pro-immigrant actions, likely setting the stage for greater state-local conflict on a variety of immigration and integration issues. SB4 will continue to restrict local-level protections for undocumented immigrants. In California, the state's robust philanthropy infrastructure played a key role in mobilizing advocates against legislation like Proposition 187. Yet Houston's philanthropic organizations are smaller, more conservative, and warier of supporting politically controversial immigration issues. Compared to local foundations in other immigrant hubs like California and New York, for example, Houston foundations supporting immigrant communities are fewer and tend to have more modest budgets. Aside from matching local funding for DACA implementation and naturalization, national funders have not generally prioritized Houston. Meanwhile, restrictionist federal and state laws—while mobilizing advocates to fight for immigrant rights locally—will continue to siphon resources from efforts to promote services and policies that can advance immigrant rights in Houston.

Houston's Changing Context and the Future of Immigrant Rights

Beyond the federal and state policy contexts, Houston's city and regional contexts will also continue to shape local immigrant rights efforts. Three key transformations will be relevant: Houston's changing demography, contentious local politics in the city of Houston and Harris County, and the civic infrastructure across the Houston metropolitan region.

Houston's Changing Demography

International migration will continue to drive population changes in Houston. As other major U.S. cities face substantial population losses, the Houston metropolitan region continues to grow rapidly—adding nearly 70,000 new residents between July 2020 and July 2021 alone, boosting its population to 7.2 million (González Kelly 2022). As the immigrant population grows, and as the children of immigrants enter schools, the workforce, and the ranks of voters, local policies and programs will need to keep up. This will be challenging in a highly unequal city that already struggles to provide educational resources to underserved neighborhoods (Cisneros et al. 2021) and where population growth is also happening in new areas of the metropolitan region. While the city of Houston and Harris County experienced the region's fastest population growth until recently, today the rise is most dramatic in suburban counties, notably Fort Bend County (southwest of Houston) and Montgomery County (north of Houston) (Fulton 2021). Given projections that the region's foreign-born population will double between 2015 and 2036, this suburbanization of population growth will dramatically diversify Houston's suburbs as well (CHF 2019), making immigrant integration issues regional—and not only urban—concerns.

A moderate population growth scenario by the GHP, Houston's largest chamber of commerce, projects that the region's White population will decrease from 39.5 percent of the total population in 2010 to 26 percent in 2040. During this 30-year period, the Black population share will also decline, though more modestly from 16.8 percent to 14.8 percent. By contrast, the largely immigrant Asian population share will increase from 8.2 percent to 11.2 percent, and the increasingly native-born Hispanic population share will rise from 35.4 percent to 48 percent, with Hispanics outnumbering all other ethnic groups combined in metropolitan Houston by 2045 (GHP 2017). The region is thus on a steady march toward a predominantly Hispanic population with a diverse share of other ethnic and racial groups. This growing diversity will enrich the region but will have profound implications for a range of issues including the economy, education, housing, transportation, and political representation.

The inequities that Hispanic immigrants currently face offer sober prospects for the future of the region's Hispanic-majority population. Most of today's Hispanic immigrants to Houston, for example, arrive with low levels of formal education, with 66 percent of Mexicans, 70 percent of Salvadorans, and 55 percent of other Central Americans lacking a high school diploma. These relatively low educational levels reflect deep inequities in many origin countries, rooted deeply in troubled colonial histories, contemporary political corruption, and U.S. political and economic intervention. They typically persist, with about half of the second- and third-generation descendants of Hispanic immigrants reporting they never attended college (Klineberg 2020a). This has implications for economic mobility, even for long-established migrants, with few opportunities to ascend out of low-paying and often dangerous jobs. In Houston, foreign-born Hispanics who have resided in the United States for 20 or more years are as likely as recent arrivals to work in low-wage jobs or as day laborers (Klineberg 2020a). Policy interventions that facilitate immigrant integration, boost educational attainment, widen access to good jobs, raise living standards, and limit the ability of businesses to exploit immigrant labor will thus remain urgent.

Houston has begun to lay a foundation for advancing immigrant rights. The city's Office of New Americans and Immigrant Communities, for example, works to facilitate immigrants' civic and sociocultural integration through a language-access program and monthly citizenship forums. HILSC has created a strong legal services support network for undocumented immigrants facing deportation, asylum seekers, and immigrants impacted by natural disasters and public health crises. However, more policy interventions are needed—both in Houston and the suburbs ringing the city—to offer supports and mitigate educational and employment disadvantages that could fuel the growth of a new underclass (Klineberg 2020a). Particularly, local immigrant rights policies need to focus on educational opportunities, economic empowerment, and civic engagement (CHF 2019). Given that Houston lags behind its peer gateway cities in health insurance coverage for immigrants (NAE 2018), greater policy attention should also be paid to strengthening access to medical care and other social services. Many of these resources will almost certainly be allocated to Houston's urban core, but the region's changing demography will necessitate greater regional coordination and investments to address growing suburban poverty and isolation.

Houston's Changing Politics

The future of immigrant rights in Houston also depends on the appetite of local policymakers to engage with the needs and interests of their diversifying population in an inclusive way. Houston's Office of New Americans and

Immigrant Communities is small and has maintained a largely apolitical stance on immigrant rights issues in order to survive, focusing on promoting naturalization, making referrals to HILSC, and financially empowering immigrants (ONAIC 2022). Local representatives, who tend to embrace a small government ethos, largely oppose broader public investments in immigrant integration, believing that instead nongovernmental organizations should fund and promote it. Many also aspire to run for higher elected office, which makes them cautious to espouse support for local immigrant rights policies that go against state and federal trends in immigration policy.

While officials representing Houston at the state and federal levels will likely remain Republican (or Republican leaning) for some time, Democrats likely will gain ground in local politics. Democrats tend to be more accommodating of immigrants and supportive of using government policy and public funding to support immigrant integration initiatives, though bipartisan support will be necessary to advance immigrant rights. Equally important in these efforts is the ability of the city council to attract a cadre of leaders who represent the city's racial and ethnic diversity. Houston's city council—which has 11 district and 5 at-large seats—currently lacks a deep bench of Hispanic and Asian officials interested in addressing immigrant rights. The city council elected in 2023 includes seven Black members, no Asian officials, and three Hispanic representatives in a city whose population is 7 percent Asian and 45 percent Hispanic. Council elections are nonpartisan and held off cycle, which tends to depress turnout and poses a challenge to diversifying local political representation. Electoral reforms and new naturalization and get-out-the vote initiatives will be needed to boost participation among the city's disproportionate number of noncitizens.

Dismayed that until recently only two Hispanics had ever been elected to Houston's at-large city council districts,[1] local civic leaders have pushed for local electoral reforms. In December 2022, the Houston chapter of LULAC filed a federal lawsuit against the city, demanding the discontinuation of at-large city council elections in Houston that they claim violate the federal Voting Rights Act. "The Latino voters of Houston have waited for fair redistricting plans," LULAC's filed court documents state. "They have waited for years for the City of Houston to end its long relationship with 'at-large' districts that dilute the electoral strength of Hispanics. The time has come to replace this old election system that functions solely to dilute the power of Houston's Latino voters" (*LULAC et al. v. City of Houston et al.*, 2022). If LULAC wins this court case, it will help address an important reason why Houston continues to suffer from notable Hispanic underrepresentation.

Savvy local political leaders have also pointed to the need for greater mentorship to stimulate a pipeline of new diverse leaders who want to run for local elected office in Houston. Promising initiatives are underway. For example, the Center for Houston's Future, created in 2000 as an affiliate of the GHP tasked with fostering diverse civic leaders, has elevated several Black leaders to office, including former mayor Sylvester Turner. Yet material support to help foster Hispanic and Asian candidates running for local elective office has been more muted (Klineberg 2020a). The Houston Hispanic Chamber of Commerce has stepped into this void, promoting student civic engagement, starting new Latino Political Action Committees, and encouraging new candidates to run for office. *Mi Familia Vota* (My Family Votes), a national civic organization focused on building Latino political power, has also had a strong presence in Houston. Still, more such leadership development initiatives are needed to close the representation gap in Houston city government, which could help boost the viability of local immigrant rights initiatives.

Houston's suburbs and outlying counties have slightly different political dynamics. Unlike Houston city council elections, Texas county elections are partisan, with candidates appearing on the ballot with their party affiliation. Republicans long dominated Harris County's five-member commissioners court, but Democrats won a three-seat majority during the 2018 "blue wave" elections during the Trump presidency. In 2022, Lina Hidalgo—the Colombian-born progressive Democrat who became Harris County judge in an upset election in 2018—narrowly won reelection against a massive Republican effort to smear her campaign, unseat her, and return Harris County to Republican control. Hidalgo beat Republican newcomer Alexandra del Moral Mealer, whose grandfather was a political refugee from the Spanish Fascist Franco regime, by only 1.6 percentage points (50.8 percent versus 49.2 percent). This is despite the fact that Mealer had won the endorsement of the *Houston Chronicle* and outspent Hildalgo four to one in what was then one of the most expensive county races in the United States (Carlton 2022; *Houston Chronicle* 2022).

Harris County's demographic transformation and recent Democratic efforts to expand voter access, along with an increase in the county's election budget from $4 million in 2016 to $33 million in 2020, help explain the critical Democratic victories of Hidalgo and others in the contested 2022 midterm elections (Harper and Platoff 2020). As of early 2024, the Harris County Commissioners Court counts four Democrats, including three Latinos and one Black official. Similarly, in Fort Bend County, population changes and an evolving electorate are resulting in more diverse slates of candidates for county office, with Democrats beginning to emerge victorious (Trovall 2022a). Democrat and Indian-born KP George, for example, was elected to serve as Fort Bend County judge in 2018—the first Asian to hold the office—and he, too, was narrowly reelected in 2022. As of early 2024, Fort Bend's five-member commissioners court counts three Democrats (up from one in 2016), including one Asian and two Black individuals.

There are early signs that the narrowing ethnoracial representation gap and the election of more Democrats to office in Houston's suburbs and outlying counties are promoting advances in immigrant rights and representation. As described in Chapter 2, Lina Hidalgo has helped funnel over $2 million to a countywide immigrant defense fund to aid immigrants facing deportation (Hansen 2020). Similarly, after the election of KP George, local civic leaders urged county officials to close schools in observance of Diwali, a popular festival of prayer among Hindus and Indians (Varma 2022). A continuing diversification of local political representation will be necessary to sustain and expand such immigrant-inclusive policy initiatives.

Additional advances in immigrant rights, whether in the city of Houston or elsewhere in the metropolitan region, will also require the engagement of immigrant youth. In recent years, they have been mobilized and activated on a range of issues. They have started organizations like FIEL, created in 2007, and a local chapter of United We Dream, created in 2008 to push for immigration reform at all levels of government, which remain major players in local immigration actions. In 2017, FIEL activists successfully pushed Houston mayor Sylvester Turner to join other cities in a lawsuit against Governor Abbott and the state of Texas over SB4 (Flores 2017). In 2022, FIEL members and their families caravanned to New Orleans to attend the hearing on the DACA program at the Fifth Circuit Court of Appeals (Taylor and Balogun 2022). Also in 2022, United We Dream activists protested outside the Houston Joint Processing Center to push Harris County officials to cut all ties with ICE (UWD 2022). Both FIEL and United We Dream have been pivotal advocates on bread-and-butter immigrant rights issues, as well as in efforts to combat racism and police brutality. Activated immigrant youth are likely to remain politically engaged over time (Terriquez and Milkman 2021), which offers hope that Houston's young population will continue to fight for immigrant rights, either in government or from within civic institutions, as they grow older.

To be sure, not all immigrants (or communities of color more broadly) uniformly support progressive immigration policies. During the late 1990s, for example, Orlando Sanchez—the conservative Cuban immigrant elected to an at-large Houston city council seat—repeatedly tried to shut down the city's immigrant affairs office. Similarly, Al Hoang—a Vietnamese immigrant who represented the immigrant-dense District F in western Houston between 2009 and 2014—argued that private sector organizations, not the city government, should promote immigrant integration. These pockets of conservatism in immigrant communities, which still exist today, have been a boon to GOP politics (Blankley 2022). The Republican Party has organized to make inroads into immigrant communities, fielding more Latino candidates during the 2022 midterm elections than before (Gardner 2022). Texas, including the diversifying Houston metropolitan region, is a place where Republicans can further develop this strategy to make gains among the state's growing number of voters of color. If they succeed, advancing immigrant rights will likely not be a policy priority of local officials, no matter how diverse city councils and county commissioners courts become.

Houston's Changing Civic Infrastructure

Finally, the future of immigrant rights in Houston depends on whether a relatively small but essential network of civic organizations can exert political pressure and garner resources to sustain and extend their supports for immigrant communities. Immigrant rights organizations are growing in number and becoming more mature and politically sophisticated, strengthening their collaborations along the way. Immigrant rights organizations that have been around for several decades—e.g., OCA–Greater Houston (1979), Boat People SOS (1980), and CRECEN (1984)—have been joined by several newer groups—e.g., the *Fe y Justicia* Worker Center (2006), FIEL (2007), United We Dream (2008), and Bonding Against Adversity (2010). This newer crop of organizations has diversified and amplified advocacy efforts and increased resources for promoting immigrant rights. Organizational efforts, however, are still concentrated in the Houston metropolitan region's urban core.

In terms of cross-organizational collaborations, several immigrant rights coalitions have emerged across the Houston metropolitan region in recent decades. These include *El Concilio Hispano de Organizaciones* (the Hispanic Council of Organizations) that supported amnesty for undocumented immigrants during the 1980s, a local chapter of the statewide Texas Immigrant Rights Coalition, the direct-action-oriented *Houston Unido* (Houston United), the faith-based Houston Coalition for Immigration Reform led by an African American pastor, and the business-driven Americans for Immigration Reform convened by the GHP and several high-profile immigration lawyers.[2] Most of these coalitions, however, have dissipated as their central campaign—the push for some type of immigration reform between the 1980s and 2000s—lost steam. More recently, in 2019, Houston Leads—a local coalition of 14 immigrant rights organizations—was created to advocate for policies that enhance the protection, safety, dignity, and inclusion of immigrants in the Houston metropolitan region (Canizales, Guttin, and Garibay 2019). It is yet unclear whether this new coalition has staying power, likely making sustained advocacy around immigration and immigrant rights issues in Houston difficult.

Some successes are notable, however. Recently, for example, the Texas Organizing Project (TOP) and other community organizations successfully advocated for Enhanced+ Library Cards across the state, including in the Harris County Public Library system, which received nearly $300,000 to implement the program. While benefitting a range of vulnerable county residents, the program especially benefits undocumented immigrants, who can use this library card as a form of photo identification needed to conduct their daily lives (Balzer 2022). TOP, founded in 2009 by former leaders of ACORN (Association of Community Organizations for Reform Now), is a 350,000-member-strong organization that focuses on direct action, grassroots lobbying, and electoral organizing to help Black and Latino working-class residents. Advancing immigrant justice has long been one of TOP's key priorities, with TOP often at the front line in Houston working with other organizations to advocate for immigrant rights. In all, immigrant rights organizations in Houston today are more diverse and stronger than two decades ago.

Labor unions in Houston complement the efforts of increasingly strong immigrant rights organizations. Together also with worker centers, they have crafted a regional strategy to rebuild labor power. Immigrant rights have remained central to labor's agenda, with some notable successes even in the business-oriented city of Houston. For example, a new partnership between the Texas Gulf Coast Area Labor Federation AFL-CIO and the Worker Defense Project—a community organization advocating for low-wage immigrant workers in Texas's construction industry—have pushed Houston and Harris County officials to address immigrant labor abuses and housing hardships (Rice 2020). Similarly, in 2019, the Texas Gulf Coast Area Labor Federation AFL-CIO collaborated with city and congressional leaders and the *Fe y Justicia* Worker Center to develop the Build Houston Better Program to ensure workplace protections and pay equity for Houston laborers and construction workers (Najarro 2019). More recently, under pressure from two major immigrant unions—UNITE-HERE! and SEIU—Mayor Sylvester Turner signed an executive order to increase the hourly minimum wage for Houston municipal employees to $15 (Office of the Mayor 2022). These wins have provided a much-needed foundation for building labor power and strengthening immigrant rights.

Simultaneously, Houston's business interests continue to play a critical role in local politics. While chambers of commerce and business associations in other cities have typically been foes in immigrant rights struggles (de Graauw 2016), business groups in Houston are critical, even if complicated, allies. Amid ongoing court challenges to DACA, several Texas business leaders have called to preserve the program, citing the economic and community benefits that DACA beneficiaries bring to the region and the state (TexasGOPVote 2022). Moreover, the GHP has been a leading supporter of these and other efforts, especially in the building trades (Steffy and Marek 2021). These business voices are critical in Houston, even if they have narrowly framed issues around economic development and are often silent on the humanitarian and social justice concerns that motivate other immigrant rights advocates. The GHP continues to host a standing Immigration Committee tasked with advocating for immigration policies that support growth and opportunity in the Houston metropolitan region (GHP 2022). These strange bedfellow collaborations will remain crucial for the future advancement of immigrant rights in Houston.

Immigration legal services providers will also continue to be in high demand. With sustained support from local foundations, notably the Houston Endowment and the Simmons Foundation, HILSC has been able to expand the services it offers. In 2020, HILSC funded 27 diverse organizations (HILSC 2021), up from 14 during its first year of grant making in 2014. Over the years, HILSC has also diversified its work. Initially, it focused on helping eligible immigrants apply for DACA and preparing others for the then-pending DAPA program. Today, it provides a much broader array of legal services, including deportation and asylum defense, and it funds organizations to conduct the forensic mental health evaluations needed in asylum cases (HILSC 2019). HILSC now also helps organizations better prepare for environmental disasters, including the hurricanes common in the region. Since the COVID-19 pandemic, it has also worked to minimize immigrant barriers to accessing public relief funds, testing, and vaccinations (HILSC 2021). Furthermore, in 2020, HILSC partnered with Houston Leads to urge Harris County officials to pass a resolution creating the Immigrant Legal Services Program, a county program that provides free legal services for Harris County residents facing deportation (RAICES 2022). These supports will be critical moving forward, regardless of whether future federal and state laws continue to focus on enforcement or perhaps also address the rights of precarious immigrant populations.

Finally, faith-based institutions will also be pivotal in the fight to advance immigrant rights in Houston. While Houstonians today are less likely to be affiliated with an organized religion, Houston is still a faith-driven city. Faith-based institutions and clergy have long been important actors in progressive movements seeking to defend civil rights, reduce economic inequalities, and welcome immigrants and refugees. This has been true across the country but especially in Houston (Klineberg 2020a). Notably, faith-based initiatives have also been central to mediate and facilitate refugee resettlement, for which Houston has historically been a hub, and to stop hate crimes against Muslim residents. When the Trump administration slashed refugee resettlement levels dramatically, faith-based institutions (i.e., Interfaith Ministries for Greater Houston) and other resettlement agencies (i.e., Refugee Services of Texas, the Alliance) had to severely limit their services to local refugees (Trovall 2022c). In late 2021, however, President Biden—after notable political pressure from members of Congress—raised the cap on refugee admissions, making Houston a top destination for thousands of Afghan evacuees practically overnight. This sudden influx stressed local organizational capacity but also helped revitalize refugee resettlement organizations, leaving them in a better position to aid future refugee arrivals.

Conclusion

While international migration will continue to shape Houston's growing population and electorate in the years to come, demographic change alone will not yield stronger immigrant rights policies and initiatives. Rather, political leadership and policies at the federal, state, and local levels will influence such advances, as will the evolving civic infrastructure in the larger Houston metropolitan region. The enduring focus on immigration enforcement at the federal and state levels may motivate some Houston city officials to continue to block immigrant rights advances. Yet a growing immigrant electorate and an expanding, maturing civil society sector will put mounting pressure on officials in the city of Houston and outlying areas to address immigrants' needs and interests in an inclusive manner. Given these factors, it is likely that while immigrant rights in Houston will continue to improve, it will be a slow and contentious process for the foreseeable future.

Conclusion

Houston's Lessons for Studying Immigrant Rights in Other Cities

Popularly nicknamed the Bayou City, Space City, and H-Town, Houston more recently has also been referred to as the Prophetic City (Klineberg 2020a). Long thought of as a Black-White southern city, sustained immigration from Latin America, Asia, and increasingly Africa has transformed Houston into one of the most ethnically and culturally diverse cities in the nation. The demographic revolution that Houston has undergone in recent decades, and how city officials and civic organizations have been responding to it, is a harbinger of national trends. Netflix's recent popular series *Mo*, set in Houston's immigrant-dense area of Alief, is also a nod to how Houston's immigrant experience resonates with the rest of the country. "This is where the American future is being worked out, and we're there first," says Stephen Klineberg, a long-time scholar of Houston, adding that "America is undergoing a phenomenal transformation, nowhere more clearly seen or more sharply articulated than in Houston" (Houston Is Home Podcast 2020). Indeed, as the fourth-largest U.S. city, with 2.3 million residents, Houston is a helpful, even if overlooked, case for understanding the local politics of immigrant integration and immigrant rights.

Immigration has long played an important role in the growth of U.S. cities and the dynamics of urban politics, but much of what we know in this regard is derived from the experiences of iconic immigrant destinations such as New York City, Los Angeles, Chicago, Boston, and San Francisco. These are cities with long migration histories, overall progressive political cultures, and well-developed infrastructures of civic organizations that can mediate the negative effects of immigration-driven diversity (e.g., Bloemraad 2006; de Graauw 2016; Foner 2000; Milkman 2006; Pallares and Flores-Gonzáles 2010). Policymakers in newer urban and suburban destinations—often places with quite different demographic, political, and civic contexts than these iconic immigrant cities—are now, or soon will be, confronting the question of how to address the needs and interests of their growing and increasingly dispersed immigrant populations (Singer 2015). Houston, a post–World War II gateway city with a rapidly diversifying, politically mixed, and organizationally underserved city context, offers valuable insights. It serves as a model for how other U.S. cities and suburbs might grapple with immigration-driven diversity and the transition to becoming fully multiethnic communities in the years to come.

This book has presented four recent case studies that reveal a slow and contentious process of advancing immigrant rights in Houston, but one that has achieved real gains despite significant challenges. The creation and precarious institutionalization of a city immigrant affairs office highlighted how a strong mayor played a key role in establishing the office and securing its survival in the face of opposition from conservative city council members. Houston succeeded in keeping federal immigration enforcement out of local policing practices even as Harris County embraced a 287(g) enforcement agreement with ICE for nearly a decade. Houston's record in implementing federal immigration benefits has been ambivalent. City officials have been willing to collaborate with local nonprofits and philanthropic organizations to promote U.S. citizenship for legal immigrants but reticent about helping undocumented youth apply for the DACA program. Finally, strange bedfellow collaborations among labor, immigrant rights, faith, and business leaders have successfully pressured business-friendly, small-government city officials to strengthen the workplace rights of immigrant workers.

These Houston case studies reveal the dynamics of advancing immigrant rights in an overall challenging federal, state, and local context, thereby providing crucial insights for scholars studying immigrant rights dynamics in other cities. Given the U.S. federal government's exclusive powers over immigration and citizenship issues (Rodríguez 2017), an enforcement-focused national policy context sets clear parameters for what city officials and local immigrant rights advocates can achieve. In Texas, the state context also has a particularly strong impact on what local immigrant rights policies and initiatives are seen as desirable, acceptable, and legal (Hessick and Chin 2014). And city-level demographic, political, and civic factors also help explain when and how Houston officials act on immigrant rights issues. Notably, the characteristics of a city's foreign-born population can determine which immigrant rights issues arise in local politics and policymaking discussions. The local government structure, the balance of partisan affiliations, the organization of local elections, and the availability of local government funding also affect local immigrant rights dynamics. Finally, the density and maturity of local civil society organizations, as well as the ability of various nongovernmental organizations to collaborate with each other and with city officials, also influence local efforts to advance immigrant rights.

How cities position themselves and respond to immigration-driven population changes is shaped partly by *national immigration policies*, which have typically been focused on immigration enforcement and not immigrant rights (Filomeno 2017). Houston city officials, Republicans and Democrats alike, have seldom resisted the enforcement-centered policies and messages emanating from Congress and the White House, often navigating a rather indeterminate course between sanctuary and enforcement. Depending on their partisan leanings, local elected leaders in other cities may be emboldened by national enforcement policies to pursue or resist these initiatives more clearly. In 2006, in Hazleton, Pennsylvania, for example, then Republican mayor Lou Barletta embraced national enforcement-first trends by championing the Illegal Immigration Relief Act, a city law that penalized renting housing to and hiring undocumented immigrants and declared English the city's official language (Longazel 2016). In Dayton, Ohio, by contrast, Independent mayor Gary Leitzell and other inclusive-minded city officials worked with community members to support a 2011 city initiative called Welcoming Dayton. In doing so, they rebuked immigrant-excluding federal enforcement policies (Housel, Saxen, and Wahlrab 2018).

Texas *state immigration politics and policies*—focused notably on immigration enforcement and racial profiling—have stifled local innovations supporting immigrant rights, especially for Houston officials who aspire to run for state (or federal) office. Republican governor Greg Abbott, for example, has aggressively sought to strengthen immigration enforcement in the state by using state resources to further militarize the Texas-Mexico border, allowing the Texas National Guard and state police to apprehend undocumented immigrants and return them to the border, halting refugee resettlement, and intimidating localities that offer sanctuary to undocumented immigrants (Goodman 2023). These state policies have drawn the ire of Houston immigrant advocates yet have endeared Abbott to his supporters, who have kept him in office since 2015. They have also made Houston city officials wary of supporting immigrant rights proposals that potentially conflict with enforcement-first state (and federal) policies. State policy contexts that are more welcoming of immigrants, including undocumented immigrants—such as those in California, New Mexico, New York, and New Jersey—can instead offer city officials encouragement, opportunities, legitimacy, and even resources to push back against national enforcement efforts and develop innovative immigrant integration policies (e.g., Colbern and Ramakrishnan 2020; Jacobson, Tichenor, and Durden 2018). There is no indication of a significant blue wave headed to Texas politics anytime soon, but Houston remains a major immigrant destination nonetheless. If and when tides do turn bluer, Houston will be primed to be an important hub of support.

City governments are subordinate to the federal and state governments, but as the institutions that actually implement policies, they do enjoy notable state-delegated powers to protect and promote the health, safety, and welfare of all city residents (de Graauw 2016). Additionally, the multilayered structure of the U.S. federal system has produced ambiguities and contradictions across agencies and jurisdictions in laws impacting immigrants, including undocumented immigrants (Provine et al. 2016; Wells 2004). This has provided openings for city officials to engage in immigrant rights policymaking, but their city's demographic, political, and civic contexts notably shape how and to what extent they do so.

The size and characteristics of a city's foreign-born population can determine the demand for and viability of certain local immigrant rights policies (Filomeno 2017). Houston has a large and diverse foreign-born population that includes many Latino, noncitizen, and undocumented immigrants. These are among the more economically and politically disadvantaged immigrants, creating the need for local education, labor, and civic engagement policies that can lift them up. Though many immigrants in Houston cannot vote, they often use other tactics—for instance, participate in demonstrations, show up at city council hearings, or start and lead immigrant advocacy organizations—to signal their needs and demands to city officials. The diversity of Houston's immigrant population also offers a cautionary tale against assuming that immigrants form a homogenized political bloc. While many of Houston's naturalized immigrants support the Democratic Party, many others are conservatives who are not necessarily supportive of expanding immigrant rights. This makes it more difficult to enact and implement local immigrant rights policies. In cities with distinct immigrant population compositions—e.g., more Asian and naturalized immigrants (e.g., San Francisco), more Muslim immigrants (e.g., Detroit), or more refugees (e.g., Atlanta)—different issues will likely surface, necessitating distinct advocacy strategies and coalitions to enact and implement immigrant rights policies.

Local government structure matters for immigration politics, with a key distinction between the mayor-council and council-manager government systems prevalent in most U.S. cities. Mayor-council systems—where an executive mayor is separately elected from the legislative council—provide mayors with notable administrative and budgetary authority as well as electoral incentives to heed immigrant demands. In contrast, council-manager systems, where the mayor is the first among equals on a council that has both legislative and executive powers, often focus on managerial efficiency rather than hot-button social issues like addressing immigrant rights (de Wilde and Nicholls 2021). Houston has a strong mayor-council system, where the mayor can create momentum critical to advancing local immigrant rights policies. Yet Houston's powerful mayors can also hold an immigrant rights issue hostage and refuse to put it on the council agenda, no matter if it has broader support from the city council. As a result, immigrant rights advocates in Houston often must target the mayor. Cities with a weak mayor-council system or a council-manager system likely require different advocacy strategies to advance immigrant rights.

The party affiliation of city officials and voters, the organization of local elections, and the availability of local government funding also deeply influence the struggle for immigrant rights. Houston is a purple city in the process of shifting from red to blue, and Democrats are slowly and consistently gaining ground. Houston's municipal elections are nonpartisan and held off cycle, which has suppressed turnout and led to a voting public that is unrepresentative of the city's diverse population (Lappie 2017). And despite a booming economy, Houston has struggled with budget deficits due to caps on its taxation power and the rising costs of the city's municipal pension system (Fulton et al. 2020). Immigrant advocates calling for larger government investments in immigrant integration thus face an uphill battle. Alternatively, cities with different partisan compositions—whether overall more Democratic or more Republican—likely offer distinct contexts for the advancement of immigrant rights. Meanwhile, cities with partisan elections that coincide with state and federal elections can elevate the visibility and importance of immigrant rights issues. And wealthier cities may have more resources to devote to costly immigrant rights policies and initiatives.

Lastly, the density and maturity of civic organizations, as well as the willingness of nongovernmental organizations to collaborate with each other and city officials, is another key part of advancing immigrant rights. Compared with other large gateway cities, Houston has relatively few civic organizations, though they are growing in number as well as becoming more mature and politically sophisticated. Along with a small and committed cadre of immigrant rights organizations and immigration legal services providers, this infrastructure is composed of several worker centers, historically weak labor unions, abundant faith-based institutions, some high-road business associations, and conservative foundations committed to promoting individual self-sufficiency. To varying degrees, all have supported immigrant integration and immigrant rights initiatives in Houston. These organizations have had a challenging time attempting to influence the local implementation of federal and state immigration policies and advocate for the enactment of local immigrant rights policies. With persistence, and occasionally by forming strategic coalitions, these organizations have realized some important wins. These include establishing a long-running program to promote citizenship among legal immigrants and securing anti-wage theft legislation also benefitting undocumented workers. Scholars studying immigrant rights dynamics in other cities will want to pay attention not only to the types of organizations engaging with immigrant rights issues but also to the process of coalition building across organizations with different missions, constituents, ideologies, goals, and resources.

The ongoing deadlock over federal immigration reform in Congress means that the most relevant arena for advancing immigrant rights may no longer be Washington, DC, but rather the many mayor's offices, legislative councils, school boards, police precincts, and union halls and other civic organizations in cities and suburbs across the country where the growing immigrant population lives and works. Consequently, we need a new way of understanding advancements in immigrant rights. We must account for how the demographic, political, and civic contexts of a place shape how and to what end immigrant rights policies and initiatives are negotiated, implemented, or stymied. This book, based on the recent experiences of Houston, provides a useful road map for thinking about how federal, state, and local contexts shape the advancement of immigrant rights and the development of inclusive multiethnic communities. With persistent international migration and volatile federal immigration politics, immigrant integration and immigrant rights will remain key governance issues for a growing number of cities and suburbs across the United States. Houston's recent experiences with advancing immigrant rights will help lead the way.

Notes

CHAPTER 1

1. All immigration data, unless otherwise noted, are taken from the American Community Survey (five-year estimates, 2017–2021).

2. Attempts to revise Houston's charter to provide for single-member council districts date back to the late 1950s but became more intense in the 1970s. With claims that the city council's at-large elections diluted minority voting strength, community activists filed an unsuccessful federal lawsuit in 1973, when Texas was not yet included under the 1965 Voting Rights Act and its 1970 amendments. Only in 1979, when federal voting rights protections finally extended to Texas (in 1975), did the U.S. Department of Justice (DOJ) enforce the provisions of the Voting Rights Act following large annexations in 1977 and 1978 that expanded Houston by about 75 square miles and brought more than 150,000 new residents—mostly White suburbanites—within city boundaries. The DOJ's lawsuit against Houston established that the city's annexations had in fact diluted minority voting percentages, and it subsequently blocked all municipal elections until the city adopted an acceptable system of representation (Thomas and Murray 1986).

3. As a result of the November 2023 municipal elections, however, three Latino men serve on the 16-member Houston city council since January 2024 (Zuvanich 2023). One represents an at-large district.

4. Small portions of the city of Houston extend into Ford Bend and Montgomery Counties.

5. Unions in states other than Texas will likely begin to experience similar resource constraints in the wake of the U.S. Supreme Court's *Janus v. AFSCME* (2018) decision limiting the collection of dues from public sector workers, who traditionally are far more likely to be unionized than private sector workers (Matthews 2018).

CHAPTER 2

1. Interview, May 24, 2012.
2. Interview, May 24, 2012.
3. Interview, May 25, 2012.
4. Interview, May 24, 2012.
5. Interview, May 24, 2012.
6. Interview, May 30, 2012.
7. Interview, June 12, 2012.
8. Interview, June 12, 2012.
9. Interview, May 30, 2012.
10. Interview, March 16, 2015.
11. Interview, July 10, 2012.
12. Interview, March 16, 2016.
13. Interview, March 16, 2016.
14. Interview, June 7, 2012.
15. Interview, June 7, 2012.
16. Interview, June 7, 2012.
17. Interview, May 30, 2012.
18. Interview, June 7, 2012.
19. Interview, July 12, 2012.
20. Interview, July 12, 2012.
21. Interview, March 16, 2016.
22. Interview, June 15, 2012.
23. Interview, March 19, 2015.
24. Interview, June 25, 2012.
25. Interviews, June 25, 2012; July 12, 2012; March 19, 2015; and March 24, 2015.
26. Interview, June 19, 2012.
27. Congressional representatives cite a number closer to 575,000 undocumented residents in the city of Houston and Harris County combined (Ortiz 2017).
28. Interview, March 4, 2015.
29. Interview, March 18, 2016.
30. Interview, March 18, 2016.
31. Interview, March 18, 2016.
32. Interview, August 2, 2016.
33. Interview, June 6, 2012.
34. Interview, June 28, 2012.
35. Interview, June 28, 2012.
36. Interview, March 10, 2015.
37. Interview, March 23, 2015.
38. Interview, June 28, 2012.
39. Interview, March 10, 2015.
40. Interview, March 19, 2015.
41. Interview, March 19, 2015.
42. Interview, March 2, 2015.
43. Interview, March 2, 2015.
44. Interview, March 13, 2015.
45. Interview, March 2, 2015.
46. Interview, March 2, 2015.

47. Interview, March 13, 2015.
48. Interview, April 7, 2016.
49. Interview, March 30, 2016.
50. Interview, March 19, 2015.
51. Interview, March 2, 2015.
52. Interview, March 13, 2015.
53. Interview, April 7, 2016.
54. Interview, March 19, 2015.

55. In the context of the United States, *notarios* are people who falsely advertise to immigrants that they can help with immigration issues and other law matters, even though they have no legal training and are not authorized to perform these legal services (Pedroza 2022).

56. Recent federal directives have reinforced the possibility of immigration relief through a process called prosecutorial discretion for unauthorized immigrants pursuing workplace claims (NILC 2023).

57. Interview, March 11, 2006.
58. Interview, July 27, 2009.
59. Interview, September 14, 2011.
60. Interview, September 23, 2011.
61. Interview, January 11, 2012.
62. Interview, September 14, 2011.
63. Interview, March 6, 2006.
64. Interview, September 16, 2011.
65. Interview, March 19, 2015.
66. Interview, March 24, 2015.
67. Interview, March 24, 2015.
68. Interview, January 11, 2012.
69. Interview, January 11, 2012.
70. Interview, July 1, 2009.
71. Interview, March 9, 2015.

72. Advocates from the Texas Gulf Coast Area Labor Federation AFL-CIO, the Worker Defense Fund, and the *Fe y Justicia* Worker Center have also pushed the Harris County district attorney to pursue cases under the 2011 Texas state law on wage theft. In the first case, a homeowner was jailed for failing to pay a contractor (Goñi-Lessan 2018). It is unclear, however, whether this enforcement mechanism has made any major strides since.

CHAPTER 3

1. A third Hispanic individual, Julian Ramirez, whose grandparents were Mexican immigrants, was narrowly elected (with 50.1 percent of the vote) to an at-large seat in a December 2023 runoff election for the Houston city council.

2. Interview, June 4, 2012.

References

Ables, Kelsey. 2022. "U.S. Judge Halts Biden Attempt to End 'Remain in Mexico' Policy." *Washington Post*, December 15, 2022. Available at https://www.washingtonpost.com/nation/2022/12/15/remain-in-mexico-policy-immigration-texas-judge.
ACS (American Community Survey). 2023a. "Selected Characteristics of the Native and Foreign-Born Populations," in 2021 5-Year Estimates, table S0501. Available at https://data.census.gov/table/ACSST5Y2021.S0501?q=S0501&g=160XX00US4835000.
———. 2023b. "Selected Characteristics of the Foreign-Born Population by Period of Entry into the United States," in 2021 5-Year Estimates, table S0502. Available at https://data.census.gov/table/ACSST5Y2021.S0502?g=160XX00US4835000.
AFL-CIO (American Federation of Labor–Congress of Industrial Organizations). 2013. "Resolution 26: Resolution to Develop a Southern Organizing Strategy [Amended]." August 26, 2013. Available at https://aflcio.org/resolutions/resolution-26-resolution-develop-southern-organizing-strategy-amended.
Ainsley, Julia. 2023. "Judge Rules against Biden Immigration Policy, Calling It 'Invalid.'" *NBC News*, July 25, 2023. Available at https://www.nbcnews.com/politics/immigration/judge-rules-biden-immigration-policy-calling-invalid-rcna96272.
Air Alliance Houston. 2021. "COVID and Public Transit in the Houston Region." October 2021. Available at https://airalliancehouston.org/wp-content/uploads/2021/10/AAH-Public-Transit-Covid-Report-final.pdf.
Allswang, John M. 1986. *Bosses, Machines, and Urban Voters*. Rev. ed. Baltimore: Johns Hopkins University Press.
Armenta, Amada. 2017. *Protect, Serve, and Deport: The Rise of Policing as Immigration Enforcement*. Oakland: University of California Press.
Arnold, Robert. 2022. "Immigration Court Backlog at 1.9 Million Cases; Attorneys Say More Resources, Law Changes Are Needed." *KPRC*, November 10, 2022. Available at https://www.click2houston.com/news/investigates/2022/11/10/immigration-court-backlog-at-19-million-cases-attorneys-say-more-resources-law-changes-are-needed.

Associated Press. 2001. "Houston Mayor Fends Off Hispanic Challenge to Win Re-election." *New York Times*, December 2, 2001. Available at https://www.nytimes.com/2001/12/02/national/houston-mayor-fends-off-hispanic-challenge-to-win-reelection.html.

Ayón, David R. 2009. *Mobilizing Latino Immigrant Integration: From IRCA to the Ya Es Hora Citizenship Campaign, 1987–2007*. Washington, DC: Woodrow Wilson International Center for Scholars, Mexico Institute.

BakerRipley. 2022. *Forward Together: 2021 Annual Report*. Houston: BakerRipley.

Balzer, Cass. 2022. "ID Made Easier." *American Libraries Magazine*, September 1, 2022. Available at https://americanlibrariesmagazine.org/?p=131336.

Binkovitz, Leah. 2017. "Could Houston Become a Protest City?" Kinder Institute for Urban Research at Rice University. January 31, 2017. Available at https://kinder.rice.edu/2017/01/31/could-houston-become-a-protest-city.

Blankley, Bethany. 2022. "Poll: Majority of Hispanic Texas Voters Say GOP Better Reflects Their Values." *Center Square*, October 7, 2022. Available at https://www.thecentersquare.com/texas/poll-majority-of-hispanic-texas-voters-say-gop-better-reflects-their-values/article_d5d8bef2-4633-11ed-a557-7f301602a33b.html.

Bloemraad, Irene. 2006. *Becoming a Citizen: Incorporating Immigrants and Refugees in the United States and Canada*. Berkeley: University of California Press.

Bloemraad, Irene, and Els de Graauw. 2012. "Diversity and Laissez-Faire Integration in the United States." In *Diverse Nations, Diverse Responses: Approaches to Social Cohesion in Immigrant Societies*, edited by Paul Spoonley and Erin Tolley, pp. 35–57. Montreal, Canada: Queen's Policy Studies Series, McGill-Queen's University Press.

BLS (U.S. Bureau of Labor Statistics). 2022. "Union Members in Texas–2021: Southwest Information Office: U.S. Bureau of Labor Statistics." 22-139-DAL. Accessed March 22, 2024. Available at https://www.bls.gov/regions/southwest/news-release/2022/unionmembership_texas_20220217.htm.

Bobo, Kim. 2008. *Wage Theft in America: Why Millions of Working Americans Are Not Getting Paid—And What We Can Do about It*. New York: New Press.

Brennan Center. 2022. "Fair Maps Texas Action Committee v. Abbott." Last updated August 18, 2022. Available at https://www.brennancenter.org/our-work/court-cases/fair-maps-texas-action-committee-v-abbott.

Bruegmann, Robert. 2008. *Sprawl: A Compact History*. Chicago: University of Chicago Press.

Canizales, Carolina, Andrea Guttin, and Julieta Garibay. 2019. "Houston Leads: Seeking Justice and Dignity for All Members of Our Community." Immigrant Legal Resource Center. July 30, 2019. Available at https://ilrc-sf.medium.com/houston-leads-seeking-justice-and-dignity-for-all-members-of-our-community-7bc7718e2478.

Capps, Randy, Michael Fix, and Chiamaka Nwosu. 2015. *A Profile of Immigrants in Houston, the Nation's Most Diverse Metropolitan Area*. Washington, DC: Migration Policy Institute.

Capps, Randy, and Ariel G. Ruiz Soto. 2018. *A Profile of Houston's Diverse Immigrant Population in a Rapidly Changing Policy Landscape*. Washington, DC: Migration Policy Institute.

Carlton, Rachel. 2022. "Alexandra del Moral Mealer Outraises Linda Hidalgo 4-to-1 for Harris County Judge Race in Final Stretch before Election Day." *Community Impact*, November 2, 2022. Available at https://communityimpact.com/houston/bay-area/election/2022/11/02/alexandra-del-moral-mealer-outraises-linda-hidalgo-4-to-1-for-harris-county-judge-race-in-final-stretch-before-election-day.

Carroll, Susan. 2009. "No Quorum Leads to No Vote on 287(g)." *Houston Chronicle*, October 29, 2009, p. B-1.

Carroll, Susan, and Chase Davis. 2008. "Elusive Justice: Thousands of Inmates Admit They're in the U.S. Illegally, but Even the Most Convicted of Violent Crimes Are Often Released Back onto Houston's Streets." *Houston Chronicle*, November 16, 2008, p. A-1.

Carroll, Susan, and Renee C. Lee. 2009. "Feds Missed Chances to Deport Suspect in Drug Raid, Police Say Houston Mayor Rips Handling of Illegal Immigrant Accused in Officer Shooting." *Houston Chronicle*, March 11, 2009, p. A-1.

Carroll, Susan, and Bradley Olson. 2009. "Who Should Get Aid from City? Comment about Citizenship Status by Mayor's Office Sets off Foes of Illegal Immigration." *Houston Chronicle*, May 17, 2009, p. B-1.

———. 2010. "Cost Sidelines Parker Promise to Use ICE Initiative at City Jail but Alternative Program Helps ID Illegal Immigrants Jails: Mayor Supports Program, but Use by City Isn't Imminent." *Houston Chronicle*, February 25, 2010, p. B-1.

CHF (Center for Houston's Future). 2019. *Houston's Economic Future: Migration—A Report on the Regional Effect of Immigration*. Houston: Center for Houston's Future.

Chishti, Muzaffar, and Jessica Bolter. 2022. *Biden at the One-Year Mark: A Greater Change in Direction on Immigration than Is Recognized*. Washington, DC: Migration Policy Institute.

Cisneros, Henry, David Hendricks, J. H. Cullum Clark, and William Fulton. 2021. *The Texas Triangle: An Emerging Power in the Global Economy*. College Station: Texas A&M University Press.

City of Houston. 2013a. "Executive Order 1-17: Language Access." Accessed March 22, 2024. Available at http://www.houstontx.gov/execorders/1-17.pdf.

———. 2013b. "Wage Theft Ordinance DC082113." Accessed March 22, 2024. Available at https://www.houstontx.gov/council/committees/pshs/20130827/wagetheftordinance.pdf.

———. 2024. "Finance Department: Wage Theft." Accessed March 22, 2024. Available at https://www.houstontx.gov/finance/wage_theft.html.

CIWO (Center for Innovation and Worker Organizing) and CLASP (Center for Law and Social Policy). 2020. "The Labor Standards Enforcement Toolbox." Rutgers Center for Innovation in Worker Organization and the Center for Law and Social Policy. September 3, 2020. Available at https://smlr.rutgers.edu/news-events/news-releases/study-wage-theft-runs-rampant-during-recessions.

Colbern, Allan, and S. Karthick Ramakrishnan. 2020. *Citizenship Reimagined: A New Framework for State Rights in the United States*. New York: Cambridge University Press.

CPPP (Center for Public Policy Priorities). 2016. "Fact Sheet: Immigrants in Houston." Accessed March 22, 2024. Available at https://everytexan.org/images/EO_2016_Fact sheet_Immigrants_HOU.pdf.

———. 2017. "Immigrants Drive the Houston Economy." March 2017. Available at https://www.houstontx.gov/na/immigration-ff/immigrants-houston-economy.pdf.

CSII (Center for the Study of Immigrant Integration at the University of Southern California). 2016. "Interactive Map: Eligible-to-Naturalize Population in the U.S." Accessed August 27, 2023. Available at https://dornsife.usc.edu/csii/eligible-to-naturalize-map.

Dahl, Robert A. 1961. *Who Governs: Democracy and Power in an American City*. New Haven, CT: Yale University Press.

de Graauw, Els. 2016. *Making Immigrant Rights Real: Nonprofits and the Politics of Integration in San Francisco.* Ithaca, NY: Cornell University Press.

———. 2018. "City Immigrant Affairs Offices in the United States: Taking Local Control of Immigrant Integration." In *The Routledge Handbook of the Governance of Migration and Diversity in Cities*, edited by Tiziana Caponio, Peter Scholten, and Ricard Zapata-Barrero, pp. 168–181. London and New York: Routledge.

———. 2021. "City Government Activists and the Rights of Undocumented Immigrants: Fostering Urban Citizenship within the Confines of US Federalism." *Antipode: A Radical Journal of Geography* 53 (2): 379–398.

de Graauw, Els, and Irene Bloemraad. 2017. "Working Together: Building Successful Policy and Program Partnerships for Immigrant Integration." *Journal on Migration and Human Security* 5 (1): 105–123.

de Graauw, Els, and Shannon Gleeson. 2021a. "Labor Unions and Undocumented Immigrants: Local Perspectives on Transversal Solidarity during DACA and DAPA." *Critical Sociology* 47 (6): 941–955.

———. 2021b. "Metropolitan Context and Immigrant Rights Experiences: DACA Awareness and Support in Houston." *Urban Geography* 42 (8): 1119–1146.

de Graauw, Els, Shannon Gleeson, and Xóchitl Bada. 2020. "Local Context and Labour-Community Immigrant Rights Coalitions: A Comparison of San Francisco, Chicago, and Houston." *Journal of Ethnic and Migration Studies* 46 (4): 728–746.

de Graauw, Els, and Floris Vermeulen. 2016. "Cities and the Politics of Immigrant Integration: A Comparison of Berlin, Amsterdam, New York City, and San Francisco." *Journal of Ethnic and Migration Studies* 42 (6): 989–1012.

Delaughter, Gail. 2022. "METRO Says Houston Transit Ridership Is Up but It's Not Back to Pre-Pandemic Levels." *Houston Public Media*, March 31, 2022. Available at https://www.houstonpublicmedia.org/articles/news/in-depth/2022/03/31/422298/metro-says-ridership-is-up-but-its-not-back-to-pre-pandemic-levels.

de Wilde, Marieke, and Walter Nicholls. 2021. "Municipal Institutions and Local Policy Responses to Immigrants: Policies towards Day Laborers in California." *Territory, Politics, Governance* 10 (3): 445–464.

DHS (Department of Homeland Security). 2023a. "DHS Announces Process Enhancements for Supporting Labor Enforcement Investigations." January 13, 2023. Available at https://www.dhs.gov/news/2023/01/13/dhs-announces-process-enhancements-supporting-labor-enforcement-investigations.

———. 2023b. "Number of Form I-821D, Consideration for Deferred Action for Childhood Arrivals, Requests by Intake and Case Status, by Fiscal Year, August 15, 2012–March 31, 2023." Accessed March 22, 2024. Available at https://www.uscis.gov/sites/default/files/document/data/DACA_performancedata_fy2023_qtr2.pdf.

Digilov, Yan, and Yehuda Sharim. 2018. *Refugee Realities: Between National Challenges and Local Responsibilities in Houston, TX.* Houston: Kinder Institute for Urban Research at Rice University.

DON (Department of Neighborhoods). 2015. "City and Local Organizations to Help Immigrants Despite Challenges to New Policies." City of Houston, Texas, press release, February 18, 2015. Available at https://www.houstonimmigration.org/press-release-city-and-local-organizations-to-help-immigrants-despite-challenges-to-new-policies.

Douglas, Erin. 2021. "Top U.S. Environmental Regulator to Visit Houston Neighborhoods Where Black and Latino Residents Bear Brunt of Pollution." *Texas Tribune*, November 15, 2021. Available at https://www.texastribune.org/2021/11/15/EPA-Regan-Houston-pollution-visit.

Duong, Trang-Thu. 2016. "'Welcoming Houston' Is Also Deportation Capital." *TribTalk*, November 16, 2016. Available at https://www.tribtalk.org/2016/11/18/welcoming-houston-is-also-deportation-capital.

Dyer, R. A. 1996. "$100,000 Contributed to Fight Wage Boost/Restaurant Group Leads in Donations." *Houston Chronicle*, December 24, 1996, p. A-14.

EEOC (Equal Employment Opportunity Commission). 2002. "EEOC Expands Immigrant Rights Partnership to Include OSHA, DOJ, and Latin American Consulates." September 27, 2002. Available at http://www.eeoc.gov/press/9-27-02.html.

Engstrom, Richard L., and Michael D. McDonald. 1981. "The Election of Blacks to City Council: Clarifying the Impact of Electoral Arrangements on the Seats/Population Relationship." *American Political Science Review* 75 (2): 344–354.

Exner, Rich. 2018. "Cleveland Ranked 27th Population Density; Columbus 37th." Cleveland.com. May 29, 2018. Available at https://www.cleveland.com/datacentral/2018/05/cleveland_is_nations_27th_most.html.

Feagin, Joe R. 1988. *Free Enterprise City: Houston in Political and Economic Perspective*. New Brunswick, NJ: Rutgers University Press.

Fechter, Joshua. 2023. "Houston Sues State in Attempt to Block New Law That Erodes Cities' Power." *Texas Tribune*, July 3, 2023. Available at https://www.texastribune.org/2023/07/03/houston-texas-lawsuit-local-control.

Federal Reserve Bank of Dallas. 2017. "At the Heart of Texas: Houston–The Woodlands–Sugar Land." Accessed March 22, 2024. Available at https://www.dallasfed.org:443/research/heart/houston.

Filomeno, Felipe Amin. 2017. *Theories of Local Immigration Policy*. Cham, Switzerland: Palgrave Macmillan.

Flores, Kimberly. 2017. "Immigrants' Organizations Are Using Nontraditional Methods to Prepare for SB4." *Houston Chronicle*, August 24, 2017. Available at https://www.chron.com/lifestyle/calle-houston/article/Immigrants-organizations-are-using-11955930.php.

Foner, Nancy. 2000. *From Ellis Island to JFK: New York's Two Great Waves of Immigration*. New Haven, CT, and New York: Yale University Press and Russell Sage Foundation.

Freemantle, Tony. 2005. "Stricter Policy on Undocumented Immigrants Asked; Residents Want an Ordinance That Would Enforce Federal Laws." *Houston Chronicle*, December 7, 2005, p. B-4.

Fulton, William. 2020. "In Houston, Some Want to See the Mayor Lose Control—At Least Some of It." Kinder Institute for Urban Research at Rice University. December 1, 2020. Available at https://kinder.rice.edu/urbanedge/2020/12/01/houston-mayor-control-city-council-firefighters.

———. 2021. "Houston and Harris County's Long Reign of Growth May Come to an End." Kinder Institute for Urban Research at Rice University. July 14, 2021. Available at https://kinder.rice.edu/urbanedge/houston-and-harris-countys-long-reign-growth-may-have-come-end.

Fulton, William, Carlos Villegas, Kyle Shelton, Ben Griffin, and Carson Bise. 2020. *Troubled Fiscal Times: A Comparison of Revenue Sources and Service Levels for Houston, Dallas, and San Antonio*. Houston: Rice University Kinder Institute for Urban Research.

Fung, Katherine. 2022. "Is the Border More Secure under Biden than Trump? What We Know." *Newsweek*, September 16, 2022. Available at https://www.newsweek.com/us-southern-border-more-secure-joe-biden-donald-trump-1743839.

García, Uriel J. 2022. "Texas Awards $307 Million in Contracts for 14 Miles of New Border Wall." *Texas Tribune*, September 29, 2022. Available at https://www.texastribune.org/2022/09/29/texas-border-wall-contracts.

Gardner, Akayla. 2022. "GOP Has More Black, Latino Candidates Despite Trump Appeals to White Voters—Republicans Ramp Up Effort to Win Hispanic Support after Texas Upset." *Bloomberg News*, October 4, 2022. Available at https://www.bloomberg.com/news/features/2022-10-04/gop-has-more-black-latino-candidates-despite-trump-appeals-to-white-voters.

GHP (Greater Houston Partnership). 2017. *Metro Houston Population Forecast: Projections to 2050*. Houston: Greater Houston Partnership.

———. 2021. "Economy at a Glance—February 2021." April 14, 2021. Available at https://www.houston.org/houston-data/economy-glance-april-2021.

———. 2022. "Public Policy." Accessed March 22, 2024. Available at https://www.houston.org/public-policy.

Gleeson, Shannon. 2012. *Conflicting Commitments: The Politics of Enforcing Immigrant Worker Rights in San Jose and Houston*. Ithaca, NY: Cornell University Press.

———. 2013. "Shifting Agendas, Evolving Coalitions: Advocating for Immigrant Worker Rights in Houston." *WorkingUSA* 16 (2): 207–226.

———. 2014. "Means to an End: An Assessment of the Status-Blind Approach to Protecting Undocumented Worker Rights." *Sociological Perspectives* 57 (3): 301–320.

———. 2016. *Precarious Claims: The Promise and Failure of Workplace Protections in the United States*. Oakland: University of California Press.

Goñi-Lessan, Ana. 2018. "Harris County Files 1st Wage Theft Charge: Man Allegedly Refused to Pay Contractor Who Made Harvey Repairs." *Houston Chronicle*, September 8, 2018, p. A-3.

González Kelly, Sam. 2022. "Rising Houston Population Trends." *Houston Chronicle*, March 25, 2022, p. A-1.

Goodman, J. David. 2023. "Gov. Abbott's Policing of Texas Border Pushes Limits of State Power." *New York Times*, July 27, 2023. Available at https://www.nytimes.com/2023/07/26/us/texas-greg-abbott-border-migrants.html.

Grant, Alexis, and Kristen Mack. 2006. "White Says Officer's Death Sped HPD Policy Change." *Houston Chronicle*, October 2, 2006, p. A-1.

Griffith, Kati L. 2012. "Undocumented Workers: Crossing the Borders of Immigration and Workplace Law." *Cornell Journal of Law and Public Policy* 21:611–697.

Grissom, Brandi. 2010. "Adrian Garcia: The TT Interview." *Texas Tribune*, October 22, 2010. Available at https://www.texastribune.org/2010/10/22/interview-with-harris-county-sheriff-adrian-garcia.

Grodzins, Morton. 1960. "The Federal System." In *Goals for Americans: The Report of the President's Commission on National Goals*, pp. 265–286. Englewood Cliffs, NJ: Prentice-Hall.

Groves, Martha. 1993. "Houston Banks on Mayor Bob: Take Heart, Richard Riordan. Another Mogul-Turned-Politician Has Used Business Sense to Help Revive His Slumping City. But It May Not Be Easy to Follow His Lead." *Los Angeles Times*, July 31, 1993. Available at https://www.latimes.com/archives/la-xpm-1993-07-31-mn-18888-story.html.

Guerrero, Jean. 2021. "3 Million People Were Deported under Obama. What Will Biden Do about It?" *New York Times*, January 23, 2021. Available at https://www.nytimes.com/2021/01/23/opinion/sunday/immigration-reform-biden.html.

Hagan, Jacqueline Maria, and Susan Gonzalez Baker. 1993. "Implementing the U.S. Legalization Program: The Influence of Immigrant Communities and Local Agencies on Immigration Policy Reform." *International Migration Review* 27 (3): 513–536.

Haile, Gelila. 2019. "Engaging Immigrants in Houston's Complete Communities Initiatives: A Closer Look at Pedestrian and Biker Safety." Kinder Institute for Urban Research at Rice University. March 19, 2019. Available at https://kinder.rice.edu/urban edge/engaging-immigrants-houstons-complete-communities-initiatives-closer-look -pedestrian-and.

Hammer, Bettina, and Craig Kafura. 2019. "Republicans and Democrats in Different Worlds on Immigration." Chicago Council on Global Affairs. October 2019. Available at https://www.thechicagocouncil.org/sites/default/files/2020-12/report_repub licans-democrats-different-worlds-on-immigration_20191008.pdf.

Hanna, Mary. 2021. "Movement after Migration: Immigrants' Disproportionate Reliance on Public Transportation." Migration Policy Institute. March 24, 2021. Available at https://www.migrationpolicy.org/article/movement-migration-immigrants-public -transportation.

Hansen, Holly. 2020. "Harris County Funnels $2.5 Million in Taxpayer Dollars to Immigrant Defense Fund." *The Texan*, November 11, 2020. Available at https://thetexan .news/harris-county-funnels-2-5-million-in-taxpayer-dollars-to-immigrant-defense -fund.

Harden, John D. 2018. "Maps Spotlight Houston Area's Multinational Communities." *Houston Chronicle*, March 8, 2018. Available at https://www.chron.com/houston/article /Maps-illustrate-Houston-s-most-internationally-12739320.php.

Harper, Karen Brooks, and Emma Platoff. 2020. "Harris County Tried to Make Voting Easier during the Pandemic; Texas Republicans Fought Every Step of the Way." *Texas Tribune*, October 15, 2020. Available at https://www.texastribune.org/2020/10/15 /harris-county-texas-voting.

Hayduk, Ron, Kristen Hackett, and Diana Tamashiro Folla. 2017. "Immigrant Engagement in Participatory Budgeting in New York City." *New Political Science* 39 (1): 76–94.

HCSO (Harris County Sheriff's Office). 2023. "Storefront and Substations." Accessed March 22, 2024. Available at https://www.harriscountyso.org/Services/STOREFRONT SANDSUBSTATIONS.

Hegstrom, Edward. 2005. "Move for HPD Help Decried: Resolution for Local Enforcement Help Invites Racial Profiling, Say Some Council Members." *Houston Chronicle*, December 14, 2005, p. B-3.

Henthorn, Thomas C. 2018. "Building a Moral Metropolis: Philanthropy and City Building in Houston, Texas." *Journal of Urban History* 44 (3): 402–420.

Hernández-León, Rubén. 2008. *Metropolitan Migrants: The Migration of Urban Mexicans to the United States*. Berkeley: University of California Press.

Hessick, Carissa Byrne, and Gabriel J. Chin, eds. 2014. *Strange Neighbors: The Role of States in Immigration Policy*. New York: New York University Press.

HHCC (Houston Hispanic Chamber of Commerce). 2022. "Advocacy and Data." Accessed March 22, 2024. Available at https://www.houstonhispanicchamber.com/advocacy -data.

HILSC (Houston Immigration Legal Services Collaborative). 2015. *Houston Immigration Legal Services Collaborative: Community Plan, October 2014–December 2015*. Accessed March 22, 2024. Available at https://www.houstonimmigration.org/wp-content/up loads/2015/10/HILSC_community_plan_FINAL.pdf.

———. 2019. "Immigrant Rights Hotline Update on Houston ICE Raids: Despite No 'Massive' Raids Reported, Immigrant Rights Hotline Provide Know Your Rights Information and Field Calls about ICE Sightings in Houston." *Houston Immigration Legal Services Collaborative* (blog). July 18, 2019. Available at https://www.houstonimmigration.org/raids-2.

———. 2020a. "2019 Impact Report." Accessed March 22, 2024. Available at https://www.houstonimmigration.org/about-us/hilsc-annual-report.

———. 2020b. "Communities Torn Apart: The Impact of Detention and Deportation in Houston." Accessed March 22, 2024. Available at https://www.houstonimmigration.org/communitiestornapart.

———. 2020c. "COVID-19 Recovery Recommendations." Accessed March 22, 2024. Available at https://www.houstonimmigration.org/covid19recovery.

———. 2021. "2020 Annual Report." Accessed March 22, 2024. Available at https://www.houstonimmigration.org/about-us/hilsc-annual-report.

Hirsch, Barry T., and David A. Macpherson. 2022. "Union Membership and Coverage Database." Accessed March 22, 2024. Available at https://www.unionstats.com.

HIWJC (Houston Interfaith Worker Justice Center). 2008. *Abuse after the Storm: A Report on Hurricane Ike Recovery and Worker Exploitation*. Accessed March 22, 2024. Available at https://en.calameo.com/books/00001601989bd480c764f.

———. 2012. *Houston, We Have a Wage Theft Problem: The Impact of Wage Theft on Our City and the Local Solutions Necessary to Stop It*. May 2012. Available at https://stopwagetheft.files.wordpress.com/2012/05/2012-houston-wage-theft-report.pdf.

Holder, Sarah. 2023. "Texas Wrests Power from Local Governments with Sweeping New Law." *Bloomberg*, June 28, 2023. Available at https://www.bloomberg.com/news/articles/2023-06-28/texas-preemption-law-overrides-city-laws-on-workers-rights-evictions.

Hopkins, Daniel J. 2010. "Politicized Places: Explaining Where and When Immigrants Provoke Local Opposition." *American Political Science Review* 104 (1): 40–60.

Housel, Jacqueline, Colleen Saxen, and Tom Wahlrab. 2018. "Experiencing Intentional Recognition: Welcoming Immigrants in Dayton, Ohio." *Urban Studies* 55 (2): 384–405.

Houston Chronicle. 2006. "Strike a Pose: City Council Opposition to a Day Labor Center Contract and Gov. Perry's Proposal to Catch Illegal Immigrants on Camera Constitute Classic Political Posturing." June 5, 2006, p. B-6.

———. 2009. "Unwanted Burden Jail Screenings Shouldn't Shift Responsibility for Immigration Enforcement." July 17, 2009, p. B-8.

———. 2022. "Editorial: We Recommend Alexandra Mealer for Harris County Judge." October 12, 2022. Available at https://www.houstonchronicle.com/opinion/endorsements/article/mealer-hidalgo-harris-county-endorsement-17504659.php.

Houston Is Home Podcast. 2020. "Prophetic City | Houston on the Cusp of a Changing America | Stephen Klineberg." October 7, 2020. YouTube video, 31:30. Available at https://www.youtube.com/watch?v=Vz2s0YzsXCE.

HPD (Houston Police Department). 1992. "General Order 500-5: Immigration." June 25, 1992. Available at https://static.texastribune.org/media/documents/HPD_General_Order_500-5.pdf.

HTRA (Human Trafficking Rescue Alliance). 2022. "Human Trafficking Rescue Alliance of the Southern District of Texas." Accessed March 22, 2024. Available at https://htratx.org.

Huang, Xi, and Cathy Yang Liu. 2018. "Welcoming Cities: Immigration Policies at the Local Government Level." *Urban Affairs Review* 54 (1): 3–32.

Hunter, Floyd. 1953. *Community Power Structure: A Study of Decision Makers*. Chapel Hill: University of North Carolina Press.

ICE (U.S. Immigration and Customs Enforcement). 2023. "Delegation of Immigration Authority Section 287(g) Immigration and Nationality Act." Accessed March 22, 2024. Available at https://www.ice.gov/identify-and-arrest/287g.

IDRA (Intercultural Development Research Association). 2022. "IDRA Denounces Court Ruling Jeopardizing Texas' Dream Act." April 13, 2022. Available at https://www.idra.org/resource-center/idra-denounces-court-ruling-jeopardizing-texas-dream-act.

Jacobson, Robin Dale, Daniel Tichenor, and T. Elizabeth Durden. 2018. "The Southwest's Uneven Welcome: Immigrant Inclusion and Exclusion in Arizona and New Mexico." *Journal of American Ethnic History* 37 (3): 5–36.

Jargowsky, Paul A. 2002. "Sprawl, Concentration of Poverty, and Urban Inequality." In *Urban Sprawl: Causes, Consequences, and Policy Responses*, edited by Gregory D. Squires, pp. 39–72. Washington, DC: Urban Institute Press.

Jonas, Susanne, and Nestor Rodríguez. 2021. "Settlement and Transformations in Houston." In *Guatemala-U.S. Migration: Transforming Regions*, pp. 115–155. Austin: University of Texas Press.

Jones, Mark P. 2019. "Near Absence of Latinos and Asians Undermines Legitimacy of Houston City Council." *Houston Chronicle*, December 17, 2019. Available at https://www.houstonchronicle.com/opinion/outlook/article/Near-absence-of-Latinos-and-Asians-on-city-14913555.php.

Jordan, Miriam, and Eileen Sullivan. 2023. "Federal Judge Blocks Biden Administration's New Asylum Policy." *New York Times*, July 25, 2023. Available at https://www.nytimes.com/2023/07/25/us/politics/biden-asylum-policy-immigration.html.

Kalleberg, Arne L. 2011. *Good Jobs, Bad Jobs: The Rise of Polarized and Precarious Employment Systems in the United States, 1970s–2000s*. New York: Russell Sage Foundation.

Kerwin, Donald, and Evin Millet. 2022. "Charitable Legal Immigration Programs and the US Undocumented Population: A Study in Access to Justice in an Era of Political Dysfunction." *Journal of Migration and Human Security* 10 (3): 190–214.

Key, V. O., Jr. 1984. *Southern Politics in State and Nation*. Knoxville: University of Tennessee Press.

Klineberg, Stephen L. 2020a. *Prophetic City: Houston on the Cusp of a Changing America*. New York: Avid Reader Press.

———. 2020b. *The 2020 Kinder Houston Area Survey: Tracking the Changes in Public Perceptions—On the Brink of a Health Pandemic, an Economic Shutdown, and a Collapse in Oil Prices*. Houston: Kinder Institute for Urban Research at Rice University.

Klineberg, Stephen L, and Robert Bozick. 2021. *The Fortieth Year of the Kinder Houston Area Survey: Into the Post-Pandemic Future*. Houston: Kinder Institute for Urban Research at Rice University.

Klineberg, Stephen L., and Jie Wu. 2013. "Houston Area Asian Survey: Diversity and Transformation among Asians in Houston: Findings from the Kinder Institute's Houston Area Asian Survey (1995, 2002, 2011)." Kinder Institute for Urban Research at Rice University. Accessed March 22, 2024. Available at https://repository.rice.edu/items/73a3c9dc-d990-4de7-bfc0-cc1ea876063d.

Knapp, Anthony, and Igor Vojnovic. 2016. "Ethnicity in an Immigrant Gateway City: The Asian Condition in Houston." *Journal of Urban Affairs* 38 (3): 344–369.

Kragie, Andrew. 2015. "Houston Top U.S. City for Refugees." *Houston Chronicle*, September 14, 2015, p. A-1.

Kriel, Lomi. 2015. "Just How Diverse Is Houston? 145 Languages Spoken Here." *Houston Chronicle*, November 5, 2015. Available at https://www.houstonchronicle.com/news/houston-texas/article/Houstonians-speak-at-least-145-languages-at-home-6613182.php.

Lamare, James W. 2000. *Texas Politics: Economics, Power, and Policy*. 7th ed. New York: Wadsworth.

Langford, Terri. 1997. "Houston Rejects Increase in Minimum Wage: About 77 Percent Opposed the Proposal, Which Would Have Set the Highest Base Pay in the Country." *Houston Chronicle*, January 20, 1997, p. 5.

Lappie, John. 2017. *The State of Local Democracy in Houston and Harris County*. Houston: Center for Local Elections in American Politics and Kinder Institute for Urban Research at Rice University.

Lauby, Fanny. 2019. "Transportation and Immigrant Political Incorporation." *Journal of Ethnic and Migration Studies* 47 (19): 4552–4569.

Legislative Reference Library of Texas. 2023. "Legislators and Leaders: Political Party Statistics." Accessed March 22, 2024. Available at https://lrl.texas.gov/legeleaders/members/partyList.cfm.

Levin, Matt. 2015. "Houston Is Both One of the Most Diverse and Most Segregated US Cities." *Houston Chronicle*, May 1, 2015. Available at https://www.chron.com/news/houston-texas/article/Houston-is-both-one-of-the-most-diverse-and-most-6236793.php#photo-7910246.

Limehouse, Jonathan. 2022. "Supporters in Houston Call for DACA to Stay." *Houston Chronicle*, October 14, 2022, p. A-6.

Lin, Jan. 1995. "Ethnic Places, Postmodernism, and Urban Change in Houston." *Sociological Quarterly* 36 (4): 629–647.

Livingston, Abby. 2019. "Houston Has Become a Political Hotbed, and Not Just Because of Thursday's Presidential Debate." *Texas Tribune*, September 12, 2019. Available at https://www.texastribune.org/2019/09/12/houston-has-become-political-hotbed.

Longazel, Jamie. 2016. *Undocumented Fears: Immigration and the Politics of Divide and Conquer in Hazleton, Pennsylvania*. Philadelphia, PA: Temple University Press.

Luce, Stephanie. 2004. *Fighting for a Living Wage*. Ithaca, NY: Cornell University Press.

LULAC (League of United Latin American Citizens) et al. v. City of Houston et al. 2022.

Maciag, Mike. 2019. "Where Nonprofits Are Most Prevalent in America." *Governing*. Accessed March 22, 2024. Available at https://www.governing.com/archive/gov-nonprofits.html.

Marek, Stan. 2015. "Policy Change Could Bring Needed Workers Out of the Shadows." *Houston Chronicle*, October 26, 2015. Available at https://www.chron.com/opinion/outlook/article/Marek-Policy-change-could-bring-needed-workers-6587757.php.

———. 2016. "What Immigration Reality Looks Like for Workers." *Houston Chronicle*, September 21, 2016. Available at https://www.chron.com/opinion/outlook/article/Marek-What-immigration-reality-looks-like-for-9237716.php.

———. 2022. "How to Stop the Migrant Caravans That Are Headed to Texas." *Texas Monthly*, January 18, 2022. Available at https://www.texasmonthly.com/opinion/how-to-stop-caravans-migrants-texas.

Martin, Florian. 2017. "More Poor People Moving to Houston's Suburbs." *Houston Public Media*, July 31, 2017. Available at https://www.houstonpublicmedia.org/articles/news/2017/07/31/227810/more-poor-people-moving-to-houstons-suburbs.

Mathur, Suchita. 2023. "Where the 'Migration Protection Protocols' Stand, Four Years after Going into Effect." *Immigration Impact*. March 24, 2023. Available at https://immigrationimpact.com/2023/03/24/where-the-migrant-protection-protocols-stand-four-years.

Matthews, Dylan. 2018. "The Supreme Court Decision Gutting Public Sector Unions, Explained." *Vox*, June 14, 2018. Available at https://www.vox.com/2018/6/14/17437832/janus-afscme-supreme-court-union-teacher-police-public sector.

McGuinness, Dylan. 2023. "Houston Mayoral Candidates: Election Key Dates to Know and More." *Houston Chronicle*, June 20, 2023. Available at https://www.houstonchronicle.com/politics/houston/article/houston-city-elections-dates-17601201.php.

McPherson, Elizabeth. 2011. "Texas Legislature Passes Groundbreaking Wage Theft Bill." *Construction Citizen* (blog). June 9, 2011. Available at https://constructioncitizen.com/blog/texas-legislature-passes-wage-theft-bill-sb1024/1106091.

Milkman, Ruth. 2006. *L.A. Story: Immigrant Workers and the Future of the U.S. Labor Movement*. New York: Russell Sage Foundation.

MOIRA (Mayor's Office of Immigrant and Refugee Affairs). 2011. *Annual Report 2010*. Houston: MOIRA.

Mollenkopf, John, and Manuel Pastor, eds. 2016. *Unsettled Americans: Metropolitan Context and Civic Leadership for Immigrant Integration*. Ithaca, NY: Cornell University Press.

Monte, Kaitlin. 2019. "How Much Do Houston Public Officials Get Paid?" *Fox 26 Houston*, November 6, 2019. Available at https://www.fox26houston.com/news/how-much-do-houston-public-officials-get-paid.

Monyak, Suzanne. 2023. "Cut Off from DACA, New Generation Faces Uncertain Futures." *Roll Call*, July 12, 2023. Available at https://rollcall.com/2023/07/12/cut-off-from-daca-new-generation-faces-uncertain-futures.

Moran, Chris. 2010. "Sheriff Forms Citizens Panel—It Will Suggest How to Improve Illegal Immigrant Screenings at Jails." *Houston Chronicle*, May 18, 2010, p. B-2.

Morris, Mike. 2013. "Tweaked Law on Wage Theft Wins OK." *Houston Chronicle*, November 21, 2013, p. B-1.

Mudd, MaryJane. 2020. "LWV of Houston Registers More than 31,000 New Citizens to Vote in 2019." *League of Women Voters* (blog). January 22, 2020. Available at https://www.lwv.org/blog/lwv-houston-registers-more-31000-new-citizens-vote-2019.

Murray, Richard. 1997. "Power in the City: Patterns of Political Influence in Houston, Texas." In *Perspectives on Texas and American Politics*, 5th ed., edited by Kent L. Tedin, Donald S. Lutz, and Edward P. Fuchs, pp. 167–191. Dubuque, IA: Kendall Hunt Publishing.

Murthy, Hamsa. 2010. "Justice and the Foreigner: Illegal Alienage and the Dilemmas of Law and Government in Modern America." Ph.D. diss., University of California, Berkeley.

NAC (New Americans Campaign). 2014. *A Financial Analysis of Application Completion in the New Americans Campaign*. July 25, 2014. https://www.newamericanscampaign.org/wp-content/uploads/2017/04/Financial-Analysis-Full-Report.pdf.

NAE (New American Economy). 2018. "NAE Cities Index." Accessed March 22, 2024. Available at https://www.newamericaneconomy.org/cities-index.

Najarro, Ileana. 2019. "Pilot Program Seeks to Ensure Worker Safety and Pay Equity." *Houston Chronicle*, April 24, 2019, p. A-3.

NCSL (National Conference of State Legislatures). 2022. "Immigration Laws and Current State Immigration Legislation." Accessed March 22, 2024. Available at https://www.ncsl.org/research/immigration/immigration-laws-database.aspx.

NILC (National Immigration Law Center). 2021. "Department of Homeland Security's Worksite Enforcement Memorandum: What You Need to Know." November 3, 2021. Available at https://www.nilc.org/wp-content/uploads/2021/11/Website-Summary-of-Oct-2021-DHS-Worksite-Enforcement-Memo-2021-11-03.pdf.

———. 2023. "New DHS Guidance on Prosecutorial Discretion for Labor Disputes (Updated March 8, 2023)." March 8, 2023. Available at https://www.nilc.org/wp-content/uploads/2023/01/FAQ-New-DHS-Guidance-on-Prosecutorial-Discretion-for-Labor-Disputes-v-2023-01-17.pdf.

Office of the Mayor. 2022. "City of Houston to Increase Minimum Wage for Municipal, Contract, and Service-Related Employees to $15 an Hour." City of Houston, Texas, press release, February 17, 2022. Available at https://www.houstontx.gov/mayor/press/2022/minimum-wage-increase.html.

Office of the Texas Governor. 2022. "Operation Lone Star Buses More than 10,000 Migrants to Sanctuary Cities." Press release, September 9, 2022. Available at https://gov.texas.gov/news/post/operation-lone-star-buses-more-than-10000-migrants-to-sanctuary-cities.

———. 2023. "Governor Abbott Signs Sweeping Package of Border Security Legislation." Press release, June 8, 2023. Available at https://gov.texas.gov/news/post/governor-abbott-signs-sweeping-package-of-border-security-legislation.

Olivas, Michael A. 2020. *Perchance to DREAM: A Legal and Political History of the DREAM Act and DACA*. New York: New York University Press.

Olson, Bradley, and Susan Carroll. 2009a. "Backlash Grows Over Screenings for ICE at Jail." *Houston Chronicle*, May 2, 2009, p. B-1.

———. 2009b. "Council Members Try to Force Vote on Immigrant Screening." *Houston Chronicle*, October 23, 2009. Available at https://www.chron.com/news/houston-texas/article/Council-members-try-to-force-vote-on-immigrant-1726972.php.

ONAIC (Office of New Americans and Immigrant Communities). 2022. "Office of New Americans and Immigrant Communities." City of Houston, Texas. Accessed March 22, 2024. Available at https://www.houstontx.gov/na.

Ortiz, Alvaro "Al." 2017. "Sheriff Gonzalez Ends Program That Transfers Undocumented Immigrants to Government." *Houston Public Media*, February 22, 2017. Available at https://www.houstonpublicmedia.org/articles/news/2017/02/22/189009/sheriff-gonzalez-ends-program-that-transfers-undocumented-immigrants-to-government.

Pallares, Amalia, and Nilda Flores-Gonzáles. 2010. *¡Marcha! Latino Chicago and the Immigrant Rights Movement*. Chicago: University of Illinois.

Pandit, Eesha. 2016. "The Government's Cold-Blooded Anti-Immigrant Scam: How ICE Is Outsourcing Detention and Deportation to Local Police." *Salon*, May 9, 2016. Available at https://www.salon.com/2016/05/09/the_governments_cold_blooded_anti_immigrant_scam_how_ice_is_outsourcing_detention_and_deportation_to_local_police.

Pedroza, Juan Manuel. 2022. "Making Noncitizens' Rights Real: Evidence from Immigration Scam Complaints." *Law & Policy* 44 (1): 44–69.

Perez-Boston, Laura. 2013. "Houston City Council Passes Historic Wage Theft Ordinance." *Construction Citizen* (blog). November 20, 2013. Available at http://www.constructioncitizen.com/blog/houston-city-council-passes-anti-wage-theft-ordinance/1311201.

Pham, Huyen, and Pham Hoang Van. 2014. "Measuring the Climate for Immigrants: A State-by-State Analysis." In *Strange Neighbors: The Role of States in Immigration Policy*, edited by Carissa Byrne Hessick and Gabriel J. Chin, pp. 21–39. New York: New York University Press.

———. 2021. "The Immigrant Climate Index." Accessed March 22, 2024. Available at https://vpham415.github.io/ICI.
Pinkerton, James. 2007. "Day Workers Plagued by Wage Theft: Advocates Try to Recoup Pay for Victims Here as Exploitation Grows in U.S." *Houston Chronicle*, July 20, 2007, p. A-1.
———. 2009a. "Parts of ICE Plan Worry Hurtt: He Says Broad Use of Program That Checks Status of Migrants Can Impair Policing." *Houston Chronicle*, May 21, 2009, p. B-1.
———. 2009b. "Words on Fallen Officer: 'He Will Be Very Sorely Missed by Us All.' Suspect Allegedly Here Illegally." *Houston Chronicle*, June 25, 2009, p. A-1.
Politico. 2023. "Greg Abbott (R) Won the Race for Texas Governor." November 26, 2023. Available at https://www.politico.com/2022-election/results/texas/statewide-offices.
Pollin, Robert, Mark Brenner, Stephanie Luce, and Jeannette Wicks-Lim. 2008. *A Measure of Fairness: The Economics of Living Wages and Minimum Wages in the United States*. Ithaca, NY: Cornell University Press.
Pratt, Joseph. 2004. "8F and Many More: Business and Civic Leadership in Modern Houston." *Houston Review of History and Culture* 1 (2): 2–7, 31–44.
Provine, Doris Marie, Monica W. Varsanyi, Paul G. Lewis, and Scott H. Decker. 2016. *Policing Immigrants: Local Law Enforcement on the Front Lines*. Chicago: University of Chicago Press.
RAICES (Refugee and Immigrant Center for Education and Legal Services). 2022. "Launch of Harris County Immigrant Legal Services Fund." April 15, 2022. Available at https://www.raicestexas.org/2022/04/15/launch-of-harris-county-immigrant-legal-services-fund.
Ramakrishnan, S. Karthick, and Tom Wong. 2010. "Partisanship, Not Spanish: Explaining Municipal Ordinances Affecting Undocumented Immigrants." In *Taking Local Control: Immigration Policy Activism in U.S. Cities and States*, edited by Monica W. Varsanyi, pp. 73–93. Stanford, CA: Stanford University Press.
Ramsey, Ross. 2010. "A Hardline in the Sand." *Texas Tribune*, September 14, 2010. Available at https://www.texastribune.org/2010/09/14/uttt-poll-an-anti-immigrant-anti-government-mood.
———. 2021. "Texans Support Keeping 'Dreamers' in the U.S., Poll Finds." *Texas Tribune*, March 3, 2021. Available at https://www.texastribune.org/2021/03/03/texas-immigration-dreamers.
Reichley, A. James. 1992. *The Life of the Parties: A History of American Political Parties*. New York: Free Press.
Reynolds, David. 2017. "Building Power on the Texas Gulf Coast." Southern Cities Research Project. United Association for Labor Education. Accessed March 22, 2024. Available at https://static1.squarespace.com/static/5e8aaf55095a7c6f03cea452/t/5f33f5ad64211d31d006e018/1597240751760/TGCAFL-CIO+Report+10-19-2017+%281%29+%281%29.pdf.
Rice, Jen. 2020. "Housing Advocates Say Houston's Approaching an Eviction 'Doomsday.'" *Houston Public Media*, July 17, 2020. Available at https://www.houstonpublicmedia.org/articles/news/harris-county/2020/07/17/377870/houston-housing-advocates-say-were-approaching-eviction-doomsday.
Robles, Justo. 2023. "Title 42 Migration Restrictions Have Ended, but Biden's New Policy Is Tougher." *The Guardian*, May 13, 2023. Available at https://www.theguardian.com/us-news/2023/may/13/title-42-migration-biden-new-policy-tougher.

Rodrigues, Janette. 2001. "Mayor Unveils Office for Immigrant-Refugee Affairs." *Houston Chronicle*, May 20, 2001. Available at https://www.chron.com/news/houston-texas/article/Mayor-unveils-office-for-immigrant-refugee-affairs-2029575.php.

Rodríguez, Cristina. 2017. "Enforcement, Integration, and the Future of Immigration Federalism." *Journal on Migration and Human Security* 5 (2): 509–540.

Rodríguez, Cristina, Muzaffar Chishti, Randy Capps, and Laura St. John. 2010. *Program in Flux: New Priorities and Implementation Challenges for 287(g)*. Washington, DC: Migration Policy Institute.

Sandoval, Edgar, and J. David Goodman. 2022. "In Texas, a Battle for Hispanic Voters Moves to the Cities." *New York Times*, November 2, 2022. Available at https://www.nytimes.com/2022/11/02/us/texas-hispanic-voters.html.

Scherer, Jasper, and Austin Bureau. 2023. "Texas Republicans Take Their Epic Battle against Blue Cities to a New Level." *Houston Chronicle*, February 19, 2023. Available at https://www.houstonchronicle.com/politics/texas/article/texas-legislature-local-government-harris-county-17783731.php.

Selby, W. Gardner. 2010. "GOP Chair Cathie Adams Says Bill White Gave Sanctuary to Illegal Immigrants as Mayor of Houston." *PolitiFact*, March 14, 2010. Available at https://www.politifact.com/factchecks/2010/mar/14/cathie-adams/gop-chair-cathie-adams-says-bill-white-gave-sanctu.

Shelton, Kyle. 2017. *Power Moves: Transportation, Politics, and Development in Houston*. Austin: University of Texas Press.

Simpson, Andrew T. 2019. *The Medical Metropolis: Health Care and Economic Transformation in Pittsburgh and Houston*. Philadelphia: University of Pennsylvania Press.

Singer, Audrey. 2015. *Metropolitan Immigrant Gateways Revisited, 2014*. Washington, DC: Brookings Institution.

Singer, Audrey, Susan W. Hardwick, and Caroline B. Brettell, eds. 2008. *Twenty-First Century Gateways: Immigrant Incorporation in Suburban America*. Washington, DC: Brookings Institution Press.

Steffy, Loren C., and Stan Marek. 2021. *Deconstructed: An Insider's View of Illegal Immigration and the Building Trades*. College Station: Texas A&M University Press.

Steil, Justin Peter, and Ion Bogdan Vasi. 2014. "The New Immigration Contestation: Social Movements and Local Immigration Policymaking in the United States, 2000–2011." *American Journal of Sociology* 119 (4): 1104–1155.

Stewart, Melissa. 2021. "Op-Ed: Texas' Economy, Restaurant Industry Need Congressional Reform to Support Immigrant Workers." *Houston Business Journal*, December 9, 2021. Available at https://www.bizjournals.com/houston/news/2021/12/09/support-immigrant-workers.html.

Stiles, Matt. 2010. "Triblog: Houston No Sanctuary, Annise Parker Says." *Texas Tribune*, March 29, 2010. Available at https://www.texastribune.org/2010/03/29/annise-parker-houston-isnt-a-sanctuary-city.

Struthers, Silvia. 2012. "Además De La Precandidatura Presidencial, Hay Contiendas Clave a Nivel Local Que Influirán En Noviembre." *Houston Chronicle*, section *La Voz*, May 27, 2012.

TAC (Texas Association of Counties). 2023. "What Is the Difference between Sheriff, Police and Constable in Texas?" Accessed August 27, 2023. Available at https://www.county.org/About-Texas-Counties/About-Texas-County-Officials/Texas-County-Sheriff /%E2%80%8BWhat-s-the-Difference-Between-Sheriff,-Police-and.

Taylor, Brittany, and Rilwan Balogun. 2022. "FIEL, Impacted Families Travel to New Orleans to Be Present at DACA Hearing Held at 5th Circuit Court of Appeals." *KPRC*,

July 5, 2022. Available at https://www.click2houston.com/news/local/2022/07/05/watch-live-fiel-impacted-families-travel-to-new-orleans-to-be-present-at-daca-hearing-held-at-5th-circuit-court-of-appeals.

Terriquez, Veronica, and Ruth Milkman. 2021. "Immigrant and Refugee Youth Organizing in Solidarity with the Movement for Black Lives." *Gender & Society* 35 (4): 577–587.

Texas Attorney General. 2022. "AG Paxton Announces Win against City of San Antonio for Violating SB4 by Refusing to Cooperate with Illegal Immigration Enforcement Efforts." News release, April 8, 2022. Available at https://www.texasattorneygeneral.gov/news/releases/ag-paxton-announces-win-against-city-san-antonio-violating-sb4-refusing-cooperate-illegal.

Texas CRES (Commercial Real Estate Services). 2021. "Businesses Flocking to Houston's Diversity." September 6, 2021. Available at https://texascres.com/trends-and-insights/the-growth-of-flexible-office-market-in-houston-2.

TexasGOPVote. 2022. "Texas Business Leaders Urge Congress to Provide Permanent Protections for Dreamers." October 6, 2022. Available at https://www.texasgopvote.com/economy/texas-business-leaders-urge-congress-provide-permanent-protections-dreamers-0014741.

Texas Military Department. 2022. "Operation Lone Star Border Support Mission." Accessed March 22, 2024. Available at https://tmd.texas.gov/operation-lone-star-border-support-mission.

Texas Politics Project at the University of Texas at Austin. 2023. "Greg Abbott Job Approval Trend." Accessed March 22, 2024. Available at https://texaspolitics.utexas.edu/set/greg-abbott-job-approval-trend.

Thomas, Robert D., and Richard D. Murray. 1986. "Applying the Voting Rights Act in Houston: Federal Intervention or Local Political Determination?" *Publius: The Journal of Federalism* 16 (4): 81–96.

Thomas, Suja A. 2020. "The Wild, Wild West for Low Wage Workers with Wage and Hour Claims (Reviewing Llezlie L. Green, Wage Theft in Lawless Courts, 107 Cal. L. Rev. 1303 (2019))." *Jotwell: The Journal of Things We Like (Lots)*, April 9, 2020. Available at https://courtslaw.jotwell.com/the-wild-wild-west-for-low-wage-workers-with-wage-and-hour-claims.

Thompson, Derek. 2019. "How Democrats Conquered the City." *The Atlantic*, September 13, 2019. Available at https://www.theatlantic.com/ideas/archive/2019/09/brief-history-how-democrats-conquered-city/597955.

Thompson, James. 2009. "Justice Bus Rolls to Stop Wage Theft." *People's World*, November 21, 2009. Available at http://www.peoplesworld.org/justice-bus-rolls-to-stop-wage-theft.

TRAC (Transactional Records Access Clearinghouse). 2018. "Immigration and Customs Enforcement Arrests: ICE Data through May 2018." Syracuse University. Accessed March 22, 2024. Available at https://trac.syr.edu/phptools/immigration/arrest.

Trounstine, Jessica, and Melody E. Valdini. 2008. "The Context Matters: The Effects of Single-Member versus At-Large Districts on City Council Diversity." *American Journal of Political Science* 52 (3): 554–569.

Trovall, Elizabeth. 2021. "Houston Is a Top Destination for Migrant Kids: Here's What It's Like in Their Own Words." *Houston Public Media*, April 8, 2021. Available at https://www.houstonpublicmedia.org/articles/news/politics/immigration/2021/04/08/395309/houston-is-a-top-destination-for-migrant-kids-arriving-at-the-southern-border.

———. 2022a. "New Voting Bloc Emerges among State's New Citizens." *Houston Chronicle*, July 21, 2022, p. A-1.
———. 2022b. "Grants to Help Immigrants on Path to Citizenship." *Houston Chronicle*, October 2, 2022, p. A-3.
———. 2022c. "Resettling Afghans Revitalized Agencies." *Houston Chronicle*, October 9, 2022, p. A-1.
Understanding Houston. 2023. "Understanding Economic Opportunity in Houston: How Opportunity and Prosperity Flow through Our Region." Accessed March 22, 2024. Available at https://www.understandinghouston.org/topic/economic-opportunity.
Univision. 2022. "Hispanic Voters: The Majority Makers." Accessed March 22, 2024. Available at https://hispanicvote.univision.com/texas/houston.
Ura, Alexa. 2016. "There's No Shading It, Harris County Went Undeniably Blue." *Texas Tribune*, November 11, 2016. Available at https://www.texastribune.org/2016/11/11/harris-county-turned-blue.
———. 2022. "Houston's At-Large City Council Districts Deprive Latinos of Fair Representation, Lawsuit Alleges." *Texas Tribune*, December 5, 2022. Available at https://www.texastribune.org/2022/12/05/houston-city-council-elections-lawsuit.
UWD (United We Dream). 2022. "ICE Out of Harris County: Immigrant Youth and Allies Rally in Houston to Reimagine Safety and Invest in Our Communities." May 19, 2022. Available at https://unitedwedream.org/press/ice-out-of-harris-county-immigrant-youth-and-allies-rally-in-houston-to-reimagine-safety-and-invest-in-our-communities.
UWU (Unemployed Workers United) and EJC (Equal Justice Center). 2022. "Have You Even Been a Victim of Wage Theft?" Action Network. August 13, 2022. Available at https://actionnetwork.org/events/know-your-rights-wage-theft?nowrapper=true&referrer=&source=.
Varma, Juhi. 2022. "Hindu Leader Asks for Diwali School Holiday." *Houston Chronicle*, August 18, 2022, p. A-3.
Varsanyi, Monica W., ed. 2010. *Taking Local Control: Immigration Policy Activism in U.S. Cities and States*. Stanford, CA: Stanford University Press.
Varsanyi, Monica W., Paul G. Lewis, Doris Marie Provine, and Scott Decker. 2012. "A Multilayered Jurisdictional Patchwork: Immigration Federalism in the United States." *Law & Policy* 34 (2): 138–158.
Vojnovic, Igor. 2003. "Laissez-Faire Governance and the Archetype Laissez-Faire City in the USA: Exploring Houston." *Geografiska Annaler* Series B 85 (1): 19–38.
Walker, Kyle E., and Helga Leitner. 2011. "The Variegated Landscape of Local Immigration Policies in the United States." *Urban Geography* 32 (2): 156–178.
Welcoming Houston. 2017. "Welcoming Houston: Task Force Recommendations." Accessed March 22, 2024. Available at https://www.houstonimmigration.org/wp-content/uploads/2017/04/Welcoming-Houston-Task-Force-Recommendations_FINAL_01-18-17.pdf.
Wells, Miriam J. 2004. "The Grassroots Reconfiguration of U.S. Immigration Policy." *International Migration Review* 38 (4): 1308–1347.
Williams, John. 2003. "The Race for City Hall 2003: Sanchez, Opponents Split on Immigrant Aid Office." *Houston Chronicle*, October 24, 2022, p. A-29.
Wu, Bryan, Liz Hamel, Mollyann Brodie, Shoa-Chee Sim, and Elena Marks. 2018. *Hurricane Harvey: The Experiences of Immigrants Living in the Texas Gulf Coast*. San Francisco: Kaiser Family Foundation and Episcopal Health Foundation.

Zaveri, Mihir. 2018. "Lina Hidalgo, a 27-Year-Old Latina, Will Lead Harris County, Texas' Biggest." *New York Times*, November 8, 2018. Available at https://www.nytimes.com/2018/11/08/us/politics/lina-hidalgo-harris-county.html.

Zuvanich, Adam. 2023. "Voters Triple Houston City Council's Latino Representation, but Advocates Still Want Greater Equity." *Houston Public Media*, December 12, 2023. Available at https://www.houstonpublicmedia.org/articles/news/city-of-houston/2023/12/12/472159/voters-triple-houston-city-councils-latino-representation-but-advocates-still-want-greater-equity.

Index

Page numbers followed by the letter t *refer to tables. Page numbers followed by the letter* f *refer to figures.*

8F Club, 15, 27
287(g) program, 81; and Harris County Sheriff's Office, 45–48; and Houston Police Department, 16, 24, 41, 42–44; racial profiling in, 42, 44, 45

Abbott, Greg, 68–69; and DACA program, 32, 51, 68; and National Guard mobilization, 4, 23, 68, 82; on refugee resettlement, 4, 11, 23, 32, 82; and Rio Grande buoy barriers, 4, 23; and SB4 law, 75
ACORN (Association of Community Organizations for Reform Now), 77
Adams, Norman, 31
Advisory Council of International Communities (ACIC), 38, 39
advocacy for immigrant rights, 7–8, 33; business organizations in, 30, 31; coalitions in, 5, 25, 76; immigrant and faith-based organizations in, 25–26; labor unions in, 28–30; MOIRA in, 35; philanthropic organizations in, 28; reluctance in, 55; in workplace, 55–62
Afghan refugees, 79

AFL-CIO, 28, 30, 57, 58, 77, 89n72
Africa, immigrants from, 2, 8, 80
Aldine suburban area, 50
Alief area of Houston, 80
American Civil Liberties Union (ACLU), 66
Americans for Immigration Reform, 31, 76
Arizona, 4, 23, 37, 56
Asian Chamber of Commerce, 31
Asians, 2, 3, 8; advisory councils for, 19; on city council, 18, 73; in city council districts, 17, 73; as civic leaders, 15; civic organizations for, 26; as Fort Bend County judge, 74; in local elections, 74; population in Houston, 3, 8, 9, 71; segregation in housing, 13
Association of Community Organizations for Reform Now (ACORN), 77
asylum seekers, 8, 54, 66, 69, 78
Atlanta, 83

BakerRipley, 49, 53, 67
Barletta, Lou, 82
Berry, Michael, 43
Biden administration, 23, 65–68, 78–79
Black Lives Matter Houston, 47

Blacks: advisory councils for, 19; on city council, 18, 73; in city council districts, 16–17; as civic leaders, 15; in Fort Bend County, 74; on Harris County Commissioners Court, 74; philanthropic organization services to, 27; population in Houston, 2, 3, 71; segregation of housing, 12–13
Boat People SOS, 25–26, 38, 53, 67, 76
Bonding Against Adversity (BAA), 50–51, 76
border enforcement policies, 7, 68–69, 70; in Biden administration, 66, 68; buoy barriers in, 4, 23; militarization in, 4, 23, 32, 67, 68, 82; Sheriff Tommy Thomas on, 45; in Trump administration, 66
Boston, 13, 15, 19, 80
Bracero contract labor program, 9
Brown, Lee, 16, 34–36, 57
Build Houston Better Program, 77
buoy barriers in Rio Grande, 4, 23
Business Beyond Borders program, 31
business leaders and organizations, 4, 30–32, 33; and immigrant affairs offices, 38; Marek as, 1, 4, 30, 31, 60, 61; and naturalization campaigns, 51; political influence of, 15, 77–78; and Proposition A, 57; and worker rights, 55, 56–57, 60, 61
business license renewal, wage theft claims affecting, 60, 62
bus system, public, 13

California, 56, 64–65, 70, 82. *See also* Los Angeles; San Francisco
California Proposition 187, 64–65
car dependence for transportation, 12, 13
Carnegie Corporation, 50
Catholic Charities, 25, 52, 53, 54, 55, 67
Catholic Legal Immigration Network, Inc. (CLINIC), 53
CBP One smartphone app, 66
Center for Houston's Future, 74
Centers for Disease Control and Prevention (CDC), 66
Central America, immigrant population from, 9, 25, 26, 72
Central American Resource Center (CRECEN), 25, 26, 76
chambers of commerce, 4, 11, 30–31, 74
Change to Win Coalition, 28
Chicago: immigrant advocacy in, 4, 33;

34; as immigrant gateway city, 2, 4, 80; immigration benefits programs in, 49; labor unions in, 29; land area of, 12; mayor-council government in, 15; nonprofit organizations in, 4, 25; progressive culture in, 8, 80; public transit system in, 15
China, immigrant population from, 9
Citizens Assistance Office, 36
Citizenship and Immigration Forums, 36, 39, 49, 50, 67
Citizenship and Integration Grant Program, 67
citizenship and naturalization, 10*t*, 11, 12, 16, 63; collaborations supporting, 48–51; cost of filing for, 49; federal policies on, 22, 67, 68; for legal immigrants, 36, 49–51, 63, 67, 68, 81, 85; local policies on, 16, 81; MOIRA supporting, 36, 39, 49–51; possibilities for immigrants with DACA, 66; public support for path to, for undocumented immigrants, 21; resources to support, 49–51; state policies on, 22; of veterans, 70; and voter registration, 21
city council of Houston, 16–19, 81; on DAPA program, 52, 55; districts in (*see* districts of city council); elections to, 17–18, 73, 84, 87n2, 87n3, 89n1; Hispanics and Latinos on, 18, 22, 34, 73, 87n3, 89n1; in mayor-council system, 15–16, 83–84; number of members, 16, 17–18, 87n3; political party affiliation in, 3, 7, 35, 36, 39, 42, 63; underrepresentation of immigrants, 18, 73; and wage theft ordinance, 60–61
city governments, 83–84
civic context of Houston, 4–5, 24–32, 63, 82, 84–85; advisory bodies in, 19; business organizations in, 5, 30–32, 33; future trends in immigrant rights and, 64, 76–78; immigrant and faith-based organizations in, 25–26; and immigrant integration, 40; labor unions in, 5, 28–30; philanthropic organizations in, 27–28
Coalition for Humane Immigrant Rights of Los Angeles (CHIRLA), 5, 25
coalitions for immigrant rights, 5, 25, 29
college tuition financing, 4, 23, 69–70
construction industry, 9, 11; labor unions in, 28; low-wage workers in, 68, 77; Marek in, 1, 30, 31, 61; wage theft in, 57, 59, 60

consular corps, 31, 58
cooperative (or marble cake) federalism, 24
Cornyn, John, 67
council-manager systems, 83–84
COVID-19 pandemic, 12, 31, 54, 66, 78
CRECEN (Central American Resource Center), 25, 26, 76
Crenshaw, Dan, 67
criminalization of immigrants, 29, 40, 42
Cruz, Ted, 67
Cuban immigrants, 35, 75

DACA (Deferred Action for Childhood Arrivals), 16, 51–55, 81; Abbott opposition to, 32, 51, 68; assistance with applications for, 54, 78; business support of, 31; court actions concerning, 23, 32, 51–52, 66, 68, 75, 77; temporary protection from deportation in, 4, 49, 51, 66
DAPA (Deferred Action for Parents of Americans and Lawful Permanent Residents), 49, 51–55, 78
day laborers, 57, 58, 63, 72; defunding of centers for, 3, 36; wage theft affecting, 59
Dayton (OH), 82
"Death Star" law, 69
Deferred Action for Childhood Arrivals. *See* DACA
Deferred Action for Parents of Americans and Lawful Permanent Residents (DAPA), 49, 51–55, 78
Democratic Party, 8, 19–22; in California, 65; city council members in, 3, 7; on DACA/DAPA programs, 52; and federal policies, 21, 23, 52, 65–66, 67; in Fort Bend County, 74; future trends in, 64, 65; in Harris County, 4, 19–21, 74; Hispanics in, 22, 23–24; and Houston as purple city, 3, 84; Houston mayors in, 3, 7, 16, 34–40, 41, 44, 45, 57, 59; on immigration policies, 3, 4, 21; and local policies, 6, 73, 74, 75, 84; naturalized immigrants in, 83; presidential candidates in, 20f, 20–21; and state policies, 69, 70
demographic context of Houston, 1–2, 7, 8–13, 62; diversity in, 1–2, 8–9, 62, 80, 83; future trends in immigrant rights and, 64, 65, 71–72; and Harris County, 74; socioeconomic characteristics in, 9–12; in suburban sprawl, 12–13, 71

Department of Neighborhoods, 37, 39
deportation, 41; from Harris County, 46, 48; legal services in, 78; during Obama administration, 23; temporary protection from, 4, 48, 49, 51, 66, 67
DeSantis, Ron, 69
detention of immigrants, 41, 66
Detroit, 83
direct democracy process, 22
District F, 40, 42, 75
District H, 40, 45, 60
District J, 40, 60
districts of city council, 16–17, 40, 73; at-large, 16, 18, 43, 73, 87n2; map of, 17f; reorganization of, 18, 73, 87n2
Down with Wage Theft campaign, 55, 59–61
Dream Act of Texas (2001, 2005), 4, 23, 69–70
driver's licenses, 13
dual (or layer cake) federalism, 24

economy of Houston: and business organizations, 31; growth years in, 14–15, 27; and philanthropic organizations, 27; and socioeconomic opportunities, 9–12; and support of naturalization campaigns, 51
education: attainment levels in immigrant population, 10t, 11, 72; and college tuition financing for undocumented students, 4, 23, 69–70; local policies on, 72; philanthropic organizations supporting, 27, 28
El Concilio Hispano de Organizaciones (the Hispanic Council of Organizations), 76
elections: of city council members, 17–18, 73, 84, 87n2, 87n3, 89n1; in Harris County, 20–21, 23–24, 45, 74; of mayors, 15, 22; nonpartisan, 19–20, 84; presidential, 20f, 20–21, 23–24; voter turnout for, 21–22, 26, 50, 73, 84
Ellis, Mark, 42
"Ellis Island of the city," District J as, 40
El Salvador, 9, 72
Emmett, Ed, 47–48
employment: and defunding of day laborer centers, 3, 36; discrimination in, 22; and labor unions (*see* labor unions); living wage in, 57; minimum wage in, 22, 55,

employment (*continued*)
  56, 57, 77; MOIRA services related to, 35; occupations in, 10*t*, 11; rights of workers in (*see* worker rights); and right to work laws, 5, 11, 29, 56; wage theft in (*see* wage theft); and work authorization, 11, 48, 51, 66, 67–68
English language skills, 10*t*, 11, 48, 56, 82
Enhanced+ Library Cards, 76–77
environmental pollution, 12–13, 15
Equal Employment Opportunity Commission (EEOC), 58
Equal Rights Ordinance of Houston, 22

Fair Maps Texas Action Committee v. Abbott (2021), 69
Faith and Justice (*Fe y Justicia*) Worker Center, 25, 30, 59, 61, 76, 77, 89n72
faith-based organizations, 25–26, 55, 84; and future of immigrant rights, 76, 78; in New Americans Campaign, 50; in wage theft campaign, 61
Familias Inmigrantes y Estudiantes en la Lucha (FIEL), 25, 26, 47, 75, 76
federalism, 24
federal policies, 5–6, 7, 33, 40–48, 81, 82; in Biden administration, 23, 65–68, 78–79; city differences in response to, 82; and future of immigrant rights, 65–68; in hierarchical system, 3, 22–24, 83; on immigration benefits, 48–55; on labor and wages, 56, 57; in Obama administration (*see* Obama administration); stalemate in reform of, 2, 23; in Trump administration, 4, 23, 47, 65, 66, 67, 74, 78; 287(g) program (*see* 287(g) program)
Fe y Justicia (Faith and Justice) Worker Center, 25, 30, 59, 61, 76, 77, 89n72
FIEL (*Familias Inmigrantes y Estudiantes en la Lucha*), 25, 26, 47, 75, 76
Fight for a Fair Economy coalition, 59
fingerprinting, 44
Florida, 4, 69
food access, 12, 28
Ford Foundation, 54
Fort Bend County, 54, 71, 74
Foster, Charles, 30
future of immigrant rights in Houston, 64–79; federal politics in, 65–68; state politics in, 68–70

Gallegos, Robert, 22
Garcia, Adrian, 45–46
Garcia, Gilbert, 22
Garcia, Sylvia, 46, 67
General Order 500-5 on Houston police, 41, 42
gentrification, 13
George, KP, 74, 75
George Foundation, 54
Gonzalez, Ed, 40, 47, 60
governors of Texas: Abbott as (*see* Abbott, Greg); Perry as, 4, 23, 37, 43, 56
Greater Houston Partnership, 4, 30, 31, 71, 74, 76, 77–78
Greater Houston Restaurant Association, 31
Greater Houston Chamber of Commerce, 30
Green, Al, 67
Guatemala, 9
Gulfton neighborhood, 13

Harris County, 4; ICE arrest rate in, 44, 46; immigration enforcement policies of, 44–48; legal services in, 78; Metropolitan Transit Authority of, 13; philanthropic organizations in, 27; political party organizations in, 19, 20–21, 23–24, 74; population growth in, 71; presidential election results in, 20*f*, 20–21, 23–24
Harris County AFL-CIO, 28, 58
Harris County Commissioners Court, 45, 46, 47, 74
Harris County Dispute Resolution Center, 58
Harris County Public Library system, 77
Harris County Sheriff's Office, 5, 33, 45–48, 81
Harris County Small Claims Court, 58
Hazleton (PA), 82
health care, 12, 27, 28, 72
Hickman, Ron, 46–47
Hidalgo, Lina, 48, 74, 75
Hispanic Chamber of Commerce, 30–31, 74
Hispanic Council of Organizations (*El Concilio Hispano de Organizaciones*), 76
Hispanics and Latinos: as candidates in local elections, 74; in city council districts, 16–17, 73; as city council members, 18, 22, 34, 73, 87n3, 89n1; as civic leaders, 15; in Democratic Party, 22, 23–24; on Harris County Commissioners Court, 74; MOIRA services to, 34;

philanthropic organization services to, 27; population in Houston, 2, 3, 9, 71–72, 83; segregation of housing, 12–13; underrepresentation of, 41; voter turnout of, 21–22, 50

Hoang, Al, 40, 75

home rule city, 15, 22

Honduras, 9

hospitality industry, 68

housing, 10*t*, 12–13, 22, 28, 35

Houston: citizenship and naturalization in (*see* citizenship and naturalization); civic context of (*see* civic context of Houston); demographic context of (*see* demographic context of Houston); enforcement policies in (*see* immigration enforcement policies); future of immigrant rights in, 64–79; as home rule city, 15, 22; immigrant affairs office in, 34–40, 81; immigration benefits in, 48–55; integration policies in (*see* integration policies); political context of (*see* political context of Houston); as Prophetic City, 3, 80; as purple city, 3, 84; as sanctuary city, 3, 16, 36, 42, 44; as Welcoming City, 16, 39; worker rights in, 55–62

Houston Beyond ICE Coalition, 47

Houston Chronicle, 47, 61, 74

Houston Coalition for Immigration Reform, 76

Houston Economic Development Council, 30

Houston Endowment, 27, 28, 50, 52, 53, 54, 78

Houston Equal Rights Ordinance, 22

Houston Gulf Coast Building and Construction Trades Council, 28

Houston Immigration Legal Services Collaborative (HILSC), 27, 44, 52–55, 72, 73, 78

Houston Interfaith Worker Justice Center (HIWJC), 59

Houston Joint Processing Center, 75

Houston Leads coalition, 76, 78

Houston Police Department, 3, 5, 33, 48; human trafficking concerns, 38, 39; officer shot by undocumented immigrant, 16, 36, 43; response to wage theft claims, 59; in Secure Communities program, 36; in 287(g) program, 16, 24, 41, 42–44

Houston United (*Houston Unido*), 76

Houston World Trade Association, 30

human trafficking, 12, 38, 39

Hurricane Harvey, 12

Hurricane Ike, 12, 59

Hurtt, Harold, 43, 59

ICE arrest rate in Harris County, 44, 46

identification cards, 16, 77

Illegal Immigration Reform and Responsibility Act, 42

Illegal Immigration Relief Act, 82

Illinois Coalition for Immigration and Refugee Rights, 25

immigrant affairs office, 34–40, 81

Immigrant Families and Students in the Struggle (FIEL), 25, 26, 47, 75, 76

immigrant organizations, 25–26, 50, 51

Immigrants' Rights Project of ACLU, 66

Immigrant Workers Freedom Ride, 29

Immigration Acts of 1921 and 1924, 8

Immigration and Nationality Act of 1965, 8

immigrant benefits, 48–55, 81; DACA program (*see* DACA); DAPA program, 51–55, 81; naturalization and citizenship in, 48–51, 81

immigration enforcement policies, 40–48, 81, 82; at border, 4, 7, 23, 32, 66, 67, 68–69, 70, 82; and future of immigrant rights, 65–68; of Harris County, 33, 44–48; of Houston Police Department, 33, 41–44, 48; of ICE (*see* Immigration and Customs Enforcement); and integration policies compared, 7; multilevel jurisdictions in, 22–24; political party views on, 21, 65; Secure Communities program in, 36, 44; state level, 4, 40, 41, 68–69, 70, 82; 287(g) program in (*see* 287(g) program)

Immigration Forums, 36, 39, 49, 50, 67

income taxes, state policies on, 14

integration policies, 7, 9, 11; civic organizations in, 40; and enforcement policies compared, 7; federal, 23, 67; local, 16, 19, 24, 72, 73, 84; political party organizations in, 20; public funding for, 49; state-level, 69–70, 82; in Welcoming City, 16, 39

Interfaith Worker Alliance, 30

jails, 16, 43, 45, 46, 48

Janus v. AFSCME (2018), 87n5

Jones, Jesse, 27
Juárez, Benito, 34–35, 37, 39
Justice and Equality in the Workplace Partnership (JEWP), 58
Justice Bus, 30, 61
Justice for Janitors campaign, 47
Justice for Our Neighbors, 25

Kerwin, Donald, 53
Khan, M. J., 42
Kids in Need of Defense, 53
Kinder Houston Area Survey, 21
Klineberg, Stephen, 80

Labor Standards Act of 1938, 56
labor unions, 5, 28–30, 84; AFL-CIO, 28, 30, 57, 58, 77, 89n72; and future of immigrant rights, 77; membership in Houston area, 29, 56; and Proposition A, 57; resource constraints of, 29, 87n5; and right to work laws, 5, 11, 29, 56; and worker rights, 56, 57, 58
laissez-faire policies, 14–15, 40
land annexation and development, 12, 87n2
language issues, 8, 9, 10t, 11, 38, 48, 56, 82
Lanier, Bob, 41, 57
Laster, Mike, 40, 60
Latin America, 2, 3, 8, 9
Latino Political Action Committees, 74
Latinos. *See* Hispanics and Latinos
leadership development initiatives, 73–74
League of United Latin American Citizens (LULAC), 18, 73
League of Women Voters, 21
Lee, Sheila Jackson, 67
legal immigrants, naturalization and citizenship for, 36, 49–51, 63, 67, 68, 81, 85
legalization programs, 52, 66, 67, 69
legal services, 78; of business organizations, 31; in citizenship application, 49, 50, 51; of HILSC, 52–55, 72, 78; in New Americans Campaign, 50; of *notarios*, 89n55; of philanthropic organizations, 27; supporting DACA and DAPA programs, 52–55
Leitzell, Gary, 82
library cards, enhanced, 76–77
Los Angeles: consular corps in, 31; immigrant advocacy in, 8, 33, 34; labor unions in, 29; land area of, 12; mayor-council government in, 15, 18; nonprofit organizations in, 25; progressive culture in, 8, 80
LULAC (League of United Latin American Citizens), 18, 73
LULAC et al. v. City of Houston et al. (2022), 73

Marek, Stan, 1, 4, 30, 31, 60, 61
market-based approach, 14, 27
Martinez, Julian, 22
mayor-council systems, 15–16, 83–84
Mayorkas, Alejandro, 68
Mayor's Advisory Council of New Americans, 19, 39
Mayor's Advisory Council on Immigrant and Refugee Affairs (MACIRA), 35, 36, 37, 38
Mayor's Hispanic Advisory Board, 19, 34
Mayor's Office of Immigrant and Refugee Affairs (MOIRA), 16, 34–40, 49–51, 67
mayors of Houston: Brown as, 16, 34–36, 57; election of, 15, 22; and immigrant affairs office, 34–40, 81; Lanier as, 41, 57; in mayor-council system, 15–16, 83–84; Parker as, 16, 37–39, 44, 55, 59, 61; political party affiliation of, 3, 7, 45; responsibilities of, 15–16; terms of, 15; Turner as, 16, 39, 74, 75, 77; White as, 16, 36–37, 43, 44, 59
Mealer, Alexandra del Moral, 74
Memorial Assistance Ministries, 25, 53, 55
Metropolitan Organization, 61
Metropolitan Transit Authority of Harris County, 13
Mexican population in Houston, 1, 9, 18, 26, 46, 72
Mexico: and border enforcement policies (*see* border enforcement policies); and "Remain in Mexico" policy, 66
Mi Familia Vota (My Family Votes), 74
Migration Policy Institute, 53
militarization of border, 4, 23, 32, 67, 68, 82
minimum wage, 22, 55, 56, 57, 77
MOIRA (Mayor's Office of Immigrant and Refugee Affairs), 16, 34–40, 49–51, 67
Mo (Netflix series), 80
Montgomery County, 71
municipal workers, 19, 57, 59, 77; pension system for, 14, 84

Muslims, 21, 65, 78, 83
My Family Votes (*Mi Familia Vota*), 74

National Association of Latino Elected Officials (NALEO), 49–51
National Center for Charitable Statistics, 27
National Conference of State Legislatures, 70
National Guard mobilization, 4, 23, 68, 82
National Immigration Law Center, 68
National Restaurant Association, 57
natural disasters, 12, 54, 59
naturalization. *See* citizenship and naturalization
Neighborhood Centers, Inc. (NCI), 49–51
New Americans Campaign (NAC), 50
New Jersey, 82
New Mexico, 82
New York, 56, 70, 82
New York City: asylum seekers transported to, 69; consular corps in, 31; DACA/DAPA programs in, 52; immigrant advocacy in, 3, 4, 8, 33, 34; as immigrant gateway city, 2, 4, 80; immigration benefits programs in, 49; labor unions in, 29; land area of, 12; mayor-council government in, 15, 18; nonprofit organizations in, 4, 25; political party organizations in, 19; progressive culture in, 3, 8, 80; public transit system in, 13, 15
New York Immigration Coalition, 5, 25
Nicaragua, 9
9/11 terrorist attacks, 45
nongovernmental organizations, 5, 13
nonprofit organizations, 12; in citizenship program, 36, 49–51, 81; legal services of, 27, 53; number in Houston, 4, 25; philanthropic support of, 27, 28; restrictions on activities of, 26; supporting worker rights, 58
Nuchia, Sam, 41

Obama administration, 23, 24, 55; DACA program in (*see* DACA); DAPA program in, 49; naturalization during, 50; Secure Communities program in, 44
Office of Immigrant and Refugee Affairs, 16, 34–40, 49–51, 67
Office of International Communities (OIC), 37–39
Office of New Americans and Immigrant Communities, 3, 19, 39, 72–73

O'Neill, Terence, 37, 39
Open Society Foundations, 50, 54
Operation Lone Star, 68
Organization of Chinese Americans (OCA)–Greater Houston, 25, 31, 76
O'Rourke, Beto, 68

paralegal services, 53
Parker, Annise, 16, 37–39, 44, 55, 59, 61
Paxton, Ken, 69
permanent residency, 48
Perry, Rick, 4, 23, 37, 43, 56
Philadelphia, 15, 34, 69
philanthropic organizations, 27–28, 63, 70, 81; in California, 65, 70; legal services funded by, 27, 54, 55; in Welcoming City program, 39
police department of Houston. *See* Houston Police Department
political context of Houston, 3–4, 5, 14–24, 33, 63; city council in (*see* city council of Houston); future trends in immigrant rights and, 64, 65, 72–76; as home rule city, 15, 22; as laissez-faire city, 14–15, 40; mayor in (*see* mayors of Houston); party organizations and elections in, 19–22, 84; state and federal policies affecting, 2–3, 14, 22–24, 65–70
political party organizations, 19–22, 84. *See also* Democratic Party; Republican Party
pollution, 12–13, 15
population of immigrants, 1–2, 7, 8–13; countries of origin, 1–2, 3, 8, 10t, 62; diversity in, 1–2, 8–9, 62, 80, 83; future trends in, 64; growth in, 2, 8, 71; historical changes in, 8, 9; quota system on, 8; socioeconomic characteristics of, 9–12; in suburban areas (*see* suburban areas); undocumented, number of, 41, 48, 66, 67
poverty, 10t, 11, 13
presidential elections, 20f, 20–21, 23–24
Prophetic City, Houston as, 3, 80
Proposition 187 initiative in California, 64–65, 70
Proposition A on living wage, 57
prosecutorial discretion in workplace claims, 89n56
public-private collaborations, 48–55
public transit system, 13, 15

Quan, Gordon, 30, 34, 42
quota system, 8

racial profiling, 42, 44, 45, 82
rail system, public, 13
Ramirez, Julian, 89n1
referendum process, 22
Refugee Act of 1980, 8
refugees: advocacy organizations for, 26, 38; city government response to, 83; countries of origin, 1–2, 3, 8, 9; and DACA/DAPA programs, 52; faith-based institutions providing services to, 78; and MACIRA, 35; and MOIRA, 34, 36, 39; public support for citizenship, 21; resettlement of, 4, 9, 11, 23, 24, 32, 78–79, 82; during Trump administration, 4
Refugee Services of Texas, 78
"Remain in Mexico" policy, 66
Republican Party, 19–21; and business organizations, 31, 32; in California, 64–65; city council members in, 3, 7, 35, 36, 39, 42, 63; on DACA/DAPA programs, 52; and federal policies, 23, 52, 65, 67; future trends in, 65; in Harris County, 4, 19–21, 74; and Houston as purple city, 3, 84; on immigration policies, 3, 4, 21; and local policies, 73, 75–76; presidential candidates in, 20f, 20–21, 23; and state policies, 4, 23, 68–70
resettlement of refugees, 4, 9, 11, 23, 24, 32, 78–79, 82
restaurant businesses: labor unions in, 28; opposition to Proposition A, 57; support of DACA program, 31; wage theft in, 59
right to work laws, 5, 11, 29, 56
Rio Grande buoy barriers, 4, 23
Rockets basketball stadium, 57

Sanchez, Orlando, 35–36, 75
sanctuary cities: asylum seekers transported to, 69; state policies on, 4, 23, 69, 82; unofficial status of Houston as, 3, 16, 36, 42, 44
San Francisco: composition of immigrant population in, 83; DACA/DAPA programs in, 52; direct democracy in, 22; as immigrant gateway city, 2, 4, 80; immigration benefits programs in, 49; political party organizations in, 19; progressive culture in, 3, 80; public transit system in, 13, 15
Save Jobs for Houston Committee, 57
SB4 law, 4, 23, 65, 69, 70, 75
SB1024 law, 56
SB1070 law, 4, 23
Secure Communities program, 36, 44
SEIU (Service Employees International Union), 28, 30, 47, 59, 77
September 11 terrorist attacks, 45
service delivery: business organizations in, 31; collaborations in, 49–55; defunding of day laborer centers affecting, 3; immigrant affairs offices in, 35, 38; immigrant and faith-based organizations in, 25–26; suburban sprawl affecting, 12, 13
Service Employees International Union (SEIU), 28, 30, 47, 59, 77
Sessions, Jeff, 51
Sheriff's Office of Harris County, 5, 33, 45–48, 81
"show me your papers" legislation (SB1070), 4, 23
Simmons Foundation, 27, 28, 52, 54, 78
socioeconomic characteristics of immigrant population, 9–12
South Texas College of Law, 50, 53
state policies, 22–24, 81, 82–83; on enforcement, 4, 40, 41, 68–69, 70, 82; and future of immigrant rights, 68–70; on integration, 69–70, 82; on labor, 56; minimalist government philosophy in, 14; out-of-state relocation of immigrants in, 4, 69; and redistricting of state legislature, 69; right to work laws in, 5, 11, 29, 56; Rio Grande buoy barriers in, 4, 23; on sanctuary cities, 4, 23, 69, 82; SB4 law in, 4, 23, 65, 69, 70, 75; and tax revenue, 14; Texas Dream Act in, 4, 23, 69–70; on undocumented immigrants, 4, 23; on wage theft, 69, 89n72
suburban areas, 72; citizenship workshops in, 50–51; conservative counties in, 4, 24; legal services in, 53; political representation in, 74, 75; population growth in, 2, 6, 12–13, 15, 71, 81

Tahirih Justice Center, 53
tax policies, 14, 28
technology businesses, 11

Tejano, 2
Temporary Protected Status (TPS), 65
Texans for Sensible Immigration Policy, 31
Texas Dream Act (2001, 2005), 4, 23, 69–70
Texas Gulf Coast Area Labor Federation of AFL-CIO, 28, 29–30, 77, 89n72
Texas Immigrant Rights Coalition, 76
Texas Organizing Project (TOP), 76–77
Texas Regulatory Consistency Act, 69
Texas state policies. *See* state policies
Texas Workforce Commission (TWC), 56, 58, 62
Third Ward, 13
Thomas, Tommy, 45
Title 42 policy, 66
transportation issues, 12, 13, 15
Trump administration, 4, 23, 47, 65, 66, 67, 74, 78
Turner, Sylvester, 16, 39, 74, 75, 77

undocumented immigrants, 3; Abbott policies on, 4, 82; California Proposition 187 on, 64–65; college tuition and financing for, 4, 23, 69–70; criminalization of, 29, 40, 42; and DACA/DAPA programs, 4, 23, 51–55; federal policies on, 23; General Order 500-5 on, 41, 42; Houston area population of, 41, 48, 67; Houston police officer shot by, 16, 36, 43; ID cards for, 16, 77; MOIRA providing services to, 35, 36, 39; national population of, 66; path to citizenship, 21, 49–51, 66; political party views on, 21; transportation barriers for, 13; 287(g) program on (*see* 287(g) program); wage theft affecting, 57–62
United Way, 49, 52
United We Dream, 25, 26, 47, 75, 76
UNITE-HERE!, 28, 77
University of Houston Law Center Immigration Clinic, 53
Univision, 50
U.S. Board of Immigration Appeals (BIA), 53
U.S. Citizenship and Immigration Services (USCIS), 49, 50, 67
U.S. Department of Homeland Security (DHS), 56, 68

U.S. Department of Justice (DOJ), 38, 87n2
U.S. Department of Labor, 56, 58
U.S. Immigration and Customs Enforcement (ICE), 75; in Harris County, 44–48; and Houston Police Department, 43, 44; and Secure Communities program, 44; and 287(g) program, 16, 24, 43, 44, 81
U.S. Supreme Court, 51, 87n5

Vietnamese immigrants and refugees, 9, 38, 40, 75
Vietnam War, 9
voter registration, 21
voter turnout, 21–22, 26, 50, 73, 84
voting rights, 17–18, 87n2
Voting Rights Act of 1965, 17–18, 69, 73, 87n2

wages, 10*t*; living wage, 57; minimum wage, 22, 55, 56, 57, 77
wage theft, 55–62, 85; campaign against (2013), 6, 32, 33, 55–62; MOIRA concerns about, 35; state policies on, 69, 89n72
Wage Theft Ordinance, 56, 61–62, 69
Welcoming America, 39
Welcoming City, Houston as, 16, 39
Welcoming Dayton, 82
White, Bill, 16, 36–37, 43, 44, 59
"white primaries," 17
Whites, non-Hispanic: in city council districts, 16; philanthropic organization services to, 27; population in Houston, 2, 3, 71
Wilson, Pete, 64–65
women on city council, 18
work authorization, 11, 48, 51, 66, 67–68
worker centers, 3, 25, 30, 36, 77, 84
Worker Defense Fund, 89n72
Worker Defense Project, 30, 77
worker rights, 32, 55–62, 77, 81, 85; federal policies on, 68; MOIRA supporting, 35; state policies on, 69, 89n72
workplace. *See* employment

YMCA International Services, 25, 53
Young Conservatives of Texas v. University of North Texas (2022), 70

Els de Graauw is Professor of Political Science, Public Policy, and International Migration Studies at Baruch College and the Graduate Center at the City University of New York. She is the author of *Making Immigrant Rights Real: Nonprofits and the Politics of Integration in San Francisco* and coeditor of *Migrants, Minorities, and the Media: Information, Representations, and Participation in the Public Sphere.*

Shannon Gleeson is the Edmund Ezra Day Professor in the Department of Global Labor and Work at the Cornell School of Industrial and Labor Relations and Brooks School of Public Policy. She is the author or coeditor of several books, including *Conflicting Commitments: The Politics of Enforcing Immigrant Worker Rights in San Jose and Houston* and *Precarious Claims: The Promise and Failure of Workplace Protections in the United States.*